Published by
HEALTH EXCELLENCE SYSTEMS
1108 Regal Row
Manchaca, Texas 78652-0609

Printed in the United States of America

ISBN No.   1-55830-010-4   **$9.95**

DEDICATED TO

the enlightenment of humankind

that all may enjoy superb well-being

and personal exaltation

T. C. Fry

ACKNOWLEDGMENTS

I am indebted to Dr. Michael Naida, my former partner in Musical Heritage Society, for many of the jokes appearing herein. Dr. Naida hailed from Poland and Russia. His smiles and infectious humor enlivened everyone who associated with him.

Also I am indebted to Howard Malaky of Passaic, New Jersey for three of the finest jokes in this book. He also hails from Russia.

Should this book be enlarged, certainly Russia and other European countries will be tapped for their wealth of profound and meaningful humor.

T. C. Fry

About the Author

I was born in Bennington, Oklahoma in 1926. I recently returned there for a homecoming/reunion. After hearing dozens of success stories, we came to the conclusion that one of Oklahoma's main products is future Californians and Texans. I am, therefore, a Texan by choice.

Though I am a health writer and lecturer, most of the jokes related herein were added to my repertoire as a result of my 25 years in business in New Jersey and New York City. Jokes are standard fare among businessmen there. I soon became proficient at matching the mirthful offerings of salesmen, businessmen and my associates.

Though I only recall a fraction of the jokes I've heard over the years, I assure you those I remember were among the ones that stood out.

When I read Norman Cousin's celebrated book, The Anatomy of An Illness, wherein he told how he overcame a medical death sentence by laughing it up, I took jokes more seriously. Many researchers delved into the psychological and physiological bases of laughter and its beneficent impact on health. The results are in. Humor is definitely healthful!

RATIONALE
The Scientific Bases for Humor's Healthfulness

My awareness of humor's benefits prompted the title of this book. Of course, readers of Reader's Digest have long been familiar with its feature, "Laughter, The Best Medicine." Both laughing and smiling have been determined to be very healthful. I have furnished some of the references that establish the healthfulness of smiling and humor.

LAUGHTER IS, INDEED, HEALTHY!

For at least 3,000 years, laughter has been accorded a beneficent role in human health, especially in recovery from diseased conditions. We need but look at Proverbs 17:22 which states: "A merry heart doeth good like a medicine; but a broken spirit drieth the bones."

Royal courts always had jesters, "fools" and clowns to keep royal spirits high and, therefore, healthier. Recorded history and medieval writings reflect that the value of mirth, merriment, humor and laughter was known. A surgeon of the 14th century, Henri de Mondeville, observed that recovery was quicker and surer by allowing relatives and close friends to visit with the patient to tell jokes, bring cheering news, and play lovely music on instruments.

The Renaissance, the great awakening which gave rise to our age, produced Shakespeare who was always quotable on about every facet of life. He touched upon humor as well, and I'm happy to include his thoughts through the mouth of a messenger in The Taming of the Shrew: " For so your doctor hold it very meet,

Seeing too much sadness hath congeal'd your blood.

And melancholy is the nurse of frenzy,

Therefore they thought it good you hear a play,
And frame your mind to mirth and merriment
Which bears a thousand charms and lengthens life.''
While music is perhaps of equal value in aiding the suffering
to recover, it is to jokes that we now address ourselves.

Observing the needs of life appropriately includes both music
and merriment. With life's needs being well met, a happy
sickness-free life is a certain result. Though laughter's recupera-
tive role in disease is well established, it has a better role in
health--it helps keep us healthy--so healthy we never become ill
in the first place.

RESEARCH CONFIRMS VALUE OF HUMOR

Compared with the wealth of books on *"The Anatomy of
Humor,"* there is a relative dearth of books that provide humor
itself, especially truly funny jokes.

Just a few of the researches and studies done on humor were
found in the University of Texas library. Little can convey the
merits of humor in sickness and health as do the titles below:

GOLDSTEIN: Psychology of Humor

MOODY: Laugh After Laugh: The Healing Power of Humor.

JACKSONVILLE: The Power of Humor.

SIMON: Humor and Its Relationship to Perceived Health,
Life Satisfaction, and Morale in Older Adults.

HAIG: The Anatomy of Humor: Bio-psycho-social and Thera-
peutic Perspectives.

LEFCOURT: Humor and Life Stress: Antidote to Adversity.

VARIOUS AUTHORS: Handbook of Humor Research.

FISHER: Pretend the World is Funny: A Psychological Analy-
sis of Comedians, Clowns, and Actors.

FREUD: Jokes and Their Relationship to the Unconscious.

GROTJAHN: Beyond Laughter, Humor and the Subconscious.

McDOUGALL: Laughter as an Antidote to Pain.

PIDDINGTON: Pleasant Adjustment to an Unpleasant Situation.

KEITH-SPIEGEL: Conceptions of Humor

SOME OF THE MECHANISMS THAT
MAKE LAUGHTER HEALTHFUL

"That which affects the body affects the mind also." John H. Tilden, M.D.

"..emotional states can produce very real, indeed measurable, changes in the structure and function of the body." Raymond A. Moody (This is to say that the mind also affects the body either for better or worse.)

"Perhaps ultimately, and in the deepest sense, humor works by rallying, and by being a manifestation of, the will to live." Raymond A. Moody

Here it is not wise to cite the involved physiological and psychological mechanisms that make jokes funny. That would be unhealthfully boring. The books referred to previously have details in depth if that is your thing.

Perhaps the most relevant effects of humor are physical. Just as saddening emotional states arising from bad news, worries and concerns can produce melancholy and despair which adversely depress physical functions, so, too, can mirth and merriment evoke a happy, outgoing, caring and carefree response. (Upon inquiry you'll find that caring and carefree are not in contradiction to each other but complementary aspects of wholesome mental attitudes.)

When the frame of mind is made positive by humor, all physiological systems function better. When the mind is made negative by adversity and worries, the same systems become depressed in function.

When the body is subjected to severe pain, the brain secretes endorphins and enkephalins which suspend certain senses and allay suffering.

In fight or flight situations, the brain also secretes these chemicals. Further, adrenaline is secreted which instantly mobilizes the body for extraordinary performance.

Once, in saving a man's life, I jumped about 20 feet off a bridge onto an embankment, and ran to a truck that had run off the highway and plunged into a river. It was partially buried in mud and water. I crawled through the broken glass of a door, found the driver under about two feet of mud and water. I pulled his body out and quickly cleaned his nose and mouth. He began breathing. In about two minutes from the time the huge truck plunged off the roadway into the river, the driver was breathing air again. I was never aware of any injury or pain to myself. But, upon returning to the crowd that had gathered along the bridge and highway, a lady, seeing my cutup and bloody condition, my torn and ripped clothing with blood and mud caked in my hair said to me: "Mister, you're sure lucky you got out that alive."

When I was shot twice, I had an awareness of it but no pain whatsoever! Later when I was involved in an auto accident. I had passed out at the wheel because of lead the poisoning resulting from bullet shrapnel. I suffered two broken arms, broken ribs and a caved in sternum, I felt no pain. It was at least 14 hours before "rigor mortis" set in and excruciating pains beset me. Even breathing was painful for more than a day. Every movement was painful.

Endorphins and/or enkephalins are also secreted in situations of elation, euphoria and ecstasy. The joys of sexual climax or orgasm are heightened by the secretion of endorphins and other body chemicals.

When the body secretes endorphins, it may also secrete

norephenephrine. And, when it secretes norephenephrine, it may also secrete endorphins. The effects of painlessness and elevated senses of well-being of these body chemicals can last up to two days. These are the chemicals that are secreted after ten to fifteen minutes of jogging or running. The condition creates what is called "a runner's high" for runners and "a second wind" for those who experience the same effects in other sports.

Likewise, the physiological mechanisms activated by humor occasion the secretion of these mood-altering chemicals. We can feel good for hours, even a day or two, when affected by humor, hilarity, merriment, good cheer, uplifting music, touching kindness and many other happiness- engendering events.

I have read elaborate descriptions of all the physical and physiological changes that occur under the influence of laughter. Needless to say, they make dry reading. They excite no mirth. So we shall not delve further into the many healthful changes that occur under the umbrella of mirth, merriment, hilarity, jokes, laughter and fun-making.

HOW TO BRIGHTEN YOUR DAY EVERYDAY!

I've reprinted below the salient needs of life so that you may imbue your life with their magnificent beneficence. If you correctly meet the needs of life, you will be exemplary of all the virtues of which humans are capable.

As it concerns jokes, I suggest that you listen to or read one or two each day. Master at least two or three new jokes you like each week. Tell them to others as occasion arises. This fixes them in your repertoire of humor.

You'll benefit from the mirth derived from the jokes you appreciate. You'll derive even more benefit in communicating your newfound jokes to others who appreciate your sense of humor.

In the following list of needs for optimum well-being, you'll find that humor, mirth and merriment have a role.

THE NEEDS OF LIFE

Foremost among our ascertainable needs are these simple requisites:

1. **Good Air.**
2. **Pure Water.**
3. **Comfortable Temperature.**
4. **Internal and External Cleanliness.** Anything taken into the body other than its biological requirements will foul it up and lead to sicknesses, diseases and degeneration.
5. **Adequate Sleep.** Precious nerve energy is generated by the brain under the condition of sleep. As well, the recuperation of other energies and the recharging of the faculties proceeds apace.
6. **Love and Appreciation.** Loveless and unappreciated individuals are unhappy, usually lonely, often bored, and thus sink into a mire of depression and lethargy. Lack of love usually arises from poor health practices that make the individual vitiated and unhealthy, hence less than appreciable and lovable.
7. **Foods of our Natural Disposition** in their natural condition as delivered up by Nature (GOD) for our delectation, delight and nourishment. Processing, cooking and food alteration deranges and destroys nutrients, thus depriving us of vital nutrients. Additionally, toxic materials are created by cooking which impair body functions, thus giving rise to illnesses, diseases and degeneration. Of course organically-grown foods are much to be preferred. As humans are biologically frugivores, a diet predominantly of fresh ripe fruits with some fresh raw vegetables, seeds and nuts serve us best. Starchy foods that must be heated to be palatable are tertiary

foods and should not be eaten in great quantity.
8. **Vigorous Activity or Exercise.** The rewards of exercise are enormous, especially mental acuity. No one can achieve health without being fit and capable.
9. **Sunshine and Natural Light.** If you want a sunny disposition, work and play in sunlight and natural light as much as possible.
10. **Play and Recreation.** Mental and physical games do, indeed, re-create and tone up all faculties.
11. **Rest and Relaxation.** The body recuperates much of its expenditures while resting and relaxing.
12. **Emotional Poise or Stability.** Your feelings are begotten by your practices and life circumstances. Make your physical and mental conditions right--cultivate a positive, helpful, sharing and loving disposition--and your feelings will be happy, and, in fact, euphoric.
13. **Pleasant Environment.** That which is good for us is pleasant, serene and harmonious. That which is bad for us is usually ugly, upsetting and repulsive.
14. **Gregariousness.** This means belonging to a group or social circle. As we humans are social creatures, we thrive in association with others: family, friends, relatives, acquaintances, etc. No one is an island unto himself. Interacting with others about feelings, thoughts, experiences, problems, and life affairs in general is a vital life need.
15. **Security of Life and Its Means.** Unless we are secure in our persons and are reasonably assured of the needs of life for ourselves and family at the very least, insecurity results which stresses us, robs us of well-being and contributes to vitality-sapping concerns.
16. Creative, Useful Work. Humans feel good about themselves when they can fend for themselves and supply their needs by their own creative efforts.
17. **Self-Mastery or Self-Control.** If you understand what makes you and the world tick--If you have knowledge of causes and

their effects--if you sense where people are coming from, this awareness will liberate your mind and put you in control of yourself. You'll be rationally directed rather than emotionally and impulsively tugged hither and thither, most often to your great detriment.

18. **Self-determination or Personal Freedom or Individual Sovereignty.** Humans do not thrive if oppressed. They must be free in their persons from all unnatural compulsions and inhibitions.

19. **Inspiration, Motivation, Purpose and Commitment.** Aimlessness gives rise to hopelessness and dissipation. We need goals in life to achieve our highest potential.

20. **Expression of the Reproductive Instincts and Drives.**

21. **Satisfaction of the Aesthetic Senses.** This is above and beyond a pleasant environment. We require extraordinary beauty in our artistic and cultural objects.

22. **Self-Reliance or Self-Confidence.** We must feel ourselves adequate to cope with life situations.

23. **A Good Self-Image** or having **a Sense of Self-Worth.** Having a feeling of importance in the order of things contributes mightily to our sense of well-being.

24. **Mirth and Merriment.** Laughter, hilarity, humor and good fun contribute to good health. He who does not have a sense of humor has a strike against him in the game of life. Research and studies have established the great value of humor to human well-being and happiness.

25. **Music.** While this is within the realm of the aesthetic senses, the power of music which we appreciate, which arouses and inspires us, and which elicits fountains of hope and optimism, transcends the aura conjured up by aesthetic considerations.

26. **Peace, Harmony and Tranquility.** States of war, strife, turmoil, conflict and fighting disturb, distress and destroy our sense of well-being. Hence, harmony and serenity must pervade our lives.

27. **Thought, Cogitation and Meditation.** Though we have

well-developed brains, precious few of us engage in profound thought or reflection. Too many of us are given to superficial rote invocations, instead of carefully and logically considered thoughts. Too many of us operate on energy-draining emotions rather than thoroughgoing reflection which gives rise to reassuring insights, understanding and self-mastery.

28. **Smiling!** Perhaps the most contagious influence in the world is a smile! Smiling normally reflects a sense of inner contentment, happiness and wonderful well-being. A smile evidences your attitude of friendliness and caring. It communicates a warm message that engenders in others much the same feelings.

29. **Friendship and Companionship.** Really, these needs are implicit within the framework of gregariousness, and love and appreciation which have been previously touched upon. This is meant to reinforce the need for close friends and at least one companion in whom we can confide and interact with. Research shows that those happily married are healthier, friendlier, more socially aware, and longer lived than the unmarried or unhappily married.

30. **Amusement and Entertainment.** While this need is implied and impinged upon in other needs considered, it is, nevertheless, helpful to spell it out. The average Americans spends hours daily before a TV set, at the movies and as a spectator to amusing events. This can be both beneficial and demeaning. While amusement does set aside our fears, worries and adverse concerns, most of it is superficial and dissipating. Little of it inspires, motivates, exalts or involves involvement. Involving yourself in amusing and entertaining others is perhaps more wholesome than being amused. We should go for participation rather than mere spectatorship. A creative hobby in which you take pride, like musical performances, music appreciation, games, competitive sports, and many other engrossing pursuits develop us into giant personalities. Interesting pursuits absorb us as nothing else can.

They develop us so that we are more appreciated, admired and loved.

31. **Fasting!** In view of today's exigencies which stress and depress us, insufficient elimination of our own wastes arises. Fasting is a beneficent measure that enables the body to catch up on its cleansing and homework. The body is a virtual panacea under the condition of the fast. Among the many benefits begotten by the body while fasting are detoxification, restoration, resolution of almost all diseases, even if pronounced "incurable," remarkable rejuvenation and extension of a perpetually younger appearance. Fasting on occasion for two to three days with an annual fast of 14 days is like magic for all our faculties! While there are some conditions that contraindicate fasting, as a rule most of us can fast with wonderful benefits! A total of 30 to 40 days of fasting per year yields enormous benefits. Further, the practice builds profound personal discipline and control!

INTRODUCTION

Being a Texan, I am, like my Texas brethren, exceptionally fun-loving. Not only do we Texans love fun, but we make lots of mirth.

Texans have a tendency to make fun out of almost any situation. Personally, I hold, along with Norman Cousins, The Readers' Digest, and others that laughter is, indeed, "the best medicine." Extensive research has proven that laughter is very healthful.

To demonstrate the Texas propensity for humor and one-upmanship, I now relate to you a short sojourn I had in Missouri a few years ago.

My host in Missouri was continually admonishing me "to prove it" with about every statement. When I wryly observed that only dense minds failed to perceive and weigh the merits of statements on their internal truth, he proudly stated that Missouri was "the show-me state."

I rejoined with: "What a coincidence. We have the identical motto in Texas except that two of the letters are transposed. Texas is 'the show-'em state.'"

This did not impress my host a bit. So I continued with: "Texas is an enormous state. If Missouri were added to it, we'd hardly know the difference in size. Texas is so large they draw it smaller on maps so we don't get the big head down there."

This brought out a shrug as if to say "that doesn't cut any mustard with me."

So I continued: "Texas is so huge that folks in West Texas shop in Los Angeles across two states because it is closer than Houston in East Texas." Again he made a gesture that communicated "so what?"

"Look," I said, "if you travelled from Texarkana on the Northeast side of Texas and went to El Paso on the western side, you'd have gone so far that if you went east instead, you'd be in the Atlantic Ocean off South Carolina."

My host seemed to have no comprehension of the enormous distances involved. So, in frustration, I stated: "Texas is so large that if you got into a car in the center of the state and headed for the border, 24 hours later you'd still be in Texas."

"I sympathize with you brother. We have cars like that in Missouri too."

*****

We Texans take great pride in our state. Of course everything in Texas is bigger and better.

Last spring I was in a super market in Austin. As I was looking over some fruits, a lady accosted a clerk near the cantaloupe counter and asked: "Could you pick me out a melon as good as the one you got for me the other day?"

The clerk responded with "I'll try ma'am." As he assessed the melons, I overhead the lady remark: "I'm from Colorado. We grow Rocky Ford melons in Colorado, and they are the greatest."

No Texan can let anything like that pass. So I joined in with "Yes ma'am, I've eaten Rocky Ford cantaloupes, and I agree they are great. They're almost as good as Texas Pecos cantaloupes."

*****

This bit of one-upmanship is characteristic of Texans. For instance, the following reflects Texans' maneuvers to come out on top.

A Texan visited Kentucky. He got into a discussion with a Kentuckian about the merits of their respective states. The Kentuckian held forth about their beautiful horses and fast women while the Texan countered with the outstanding virtues of Texas women and horses.

Then the Texan spoke of the enormous amount of oil in Texas and how rich Texans are. This prompted the Kentuckian to boast about the enormous amount of gold stored in Ft. Knox.

"We have so much gold that we could build a solid gold fence a foot thick and three feet high all the way around the state of Texas."

"You really could do that?" asked the Texan.

"We sure could" replied the Kentuckian.

"Tell you what," said the Texan. "I love your proposal. You go ahead and build the fence. I'm going to buy it. "

*****

Texans are given to colorful language. While the following may be off-color, it nevertheless reflects the tendency.

Texas is a very oil oriented state, and terms used in the oil fields sometimes show up in common usage.

Hence, some Texas men have been known to refer to relations with their wife after menopause as "drilling in a dry hole."

*****

This is by no means a book of jokes pertaining to Texas. But it does, perhaps, acquaint you with our disposition here. We make humor out of ordinary situations. The Texas "Aggie" jokes alone would fill a volume. But most are too corny to merit our consideration here.

Most of the hundreds of jokes in this volume I picked up from others. A substantial number of these jokes have never been told or published before. Which is to say, they are original. I have read and heard thousands upon thousands of jokes. Most were rather trite and had insufficient impact to arouse uproarious laughter. I have tried to present jokes with lots of laughter potential.

This book may not strike everyone as being funny. Many let just one off-color joke ruin everything else for themselves. In fact, some of the humor may offend those of a more prudish disposition. On the other hand, most of the jokes are just plain fun--good clean fun! *Enjoy!*

THE WORLD'S FUNNIEST JOKES!

1. WE WILL NOT BE UNDERSOLD!

Lady to delicatessen owner: "Do you have any salami?"

"Yes, we have lots of it" was the reply as he led the inquirer to the salami counter.

"How much is your salami" asked the shopper.

"$5.95 per pound."

"$5.95 a pound? The delicatessen down the street offers salami at $4.25 per pound."

"Lady, if they're offering salami at $4.25 per pound, I suggest you buy it there."

"But they don't have any."

"Lady, if I didn't have any, I'd sell salami for only $2.95 per pound."

2. THE BEST OF THE BEST!

A barber in New York City situated his shop on a very busy block. Over his shop he placed a boast: "The best barber in New York City."

He became so extraordinarily busy that a second barber soon located on the same block. Not to be outdone, the second barber put a boastful sign over his shop too. It read: "The best barber in the United States."

Soon, yet another barber located on the same busy block. He, too, put a boastful sign over his shop. His sign read: "The best barber in the world."

Later, a fourth barber located his shop on this same block. He, too, put up a sign that bespoke his expertise. His sign read, very simply, "The best barber on this block."

3. I BEG YOUR PARDON. I'M NOT A DOCTOR

In Brooklyn a man went fishing from a pier near the beach. After two hours, not a single fish had bitten. So he took a walk down the pier. Soon he spotted a man with two nice-sized fish. He engaged the successful fisherman.

"Sir, did you catch those fish from this pier?"

"Indeed, I did."

"Tell me, sir, what did you use for bait?"

Come the response: "Quite frankly, I'm a physician. This morning I did a tonsillectomy on a young lad."

The seeker continued down the pier. He espied a gentleman carrying eight fair-sized fish. He accosted the fisherman.

"Did you catch those fish from this pier?"

"Yes, my good man."

"Tell me sir, what did you use for bait?"

The gentleman made this response: "To be forthright, I'm a surgeon. This morning I performed an appendectomy."

The explorer continued down the pier. A gentleman staggered toward him with perhaps twenty fish of about the same size. Despite the struggles of the fish-laden fellow, he asked: "Did you catch all those fish from this pier?"

"Yes, I did."

"Tell me, doctor, what did you use for bait?"

"I beg your pardon," the burdened fisherman responded. "I'm not a doctor. I'm a rabbi."

4. "DAMMIT, I MISSED"

A priest was an avid golfer. He golfed at every opportunity. Sometimes this was three or four times a week.

An unexpected opportunity arose. He called the golf course for a reservation. He was granted a reservation on the condition that he bring his own caddy as no caddy was available.

The priest canvassed his fellow fathers with negative results. He got a bright idea. He went over to the convent and asked if any sister would caddy for him. A sister volunteered.

After about two holes on the course, the priest was heard to exclaim: "Dammit, I missed."

"Father! Your language," protested the nun.

"I'm sorry sister. I won't do it again."

But a few holes later the father again swore: "Dammit, I missed."

The nun, quite taken aback, said: "Father, please promise me you won't say that again."

"I promise," responded the priest.

Yet a few more holes down the course, the golfing priest again swore: "Dammit, I missed."

The shocked nun sternly rebuked the padre. "Father, you promised me you wouldn't say that again. You say that again and I'll pray to our Father in heaven that he strike you dead."

"Okay, okay! I've got your message," countered the priest.

Despite this the father was heard to say, after a few more holes: "Dammit I missed."

The nun made the sign of the cross and said the prayer she said she would.

Moments later a bolt of lightning struck the nun dead. And a voice from heaven was heard to say: "Dammit, I missed."

5. BURYING YOUR DOG IN STYLE

A well-to-do rancher here in Texas went to a Baptist church in a nearby town of fair size and requested to see the minister. Upon his appearance the rancher said: "Reverend Allen, my beloved dog just died. I'd like to give him a regular burial in a cemetery with full services."

The astonished minister stammered: "We don't give services or burials for dogs."

"Well, Reverend Allen, who do you think might do this for me?"

"I suggest you try the Methodist church just a little farther down this road."

A little later the dog-lover called on the Methodist minister and made the same request.

"Sir, all our cemetery plots are for church members only. I couldn't bury your dog there even if I wanted to."

"Reverend Porter, to save me time, tell me who you think might do this for me?"

"I suggest you see Father Flanagan at the Catholic church on Pecan street on the other side of town."

Within a short time, the dog-lover was calling on Father Patrick Flanagan.

"Father Flanagan, I had a dog which I grew very fond of. My dog just died. I want to give him a regular funeral with full services. Can you do this for me?"

"God knows I'd like to do this for you. But I can only perform funeral services and bury those of our faith."

"Father Flanagan, I think I should tell you that I loved this dog so much I made a bequest of $25,

0 for funeral services and the burial costs. Further, the dog has a cemetery maintenance fund of $10.00!"

"My good man," rejoined Father Flanagan, "Why didn't you tell me your dog was Catholic?"

6. VISITING ENGLAND

In 1950 I took a trip to England aboard a Cunard passenger ship. On the trip I met an older, English gentleman who was returning home with his wife. They had visited a daughter in Iowa.

The gentleman played many games at which I was also proficient. We played darts, draughts (checkers), and chess.

He invited me to his home in Watford near London.

On the occasion of my first visit we were playing chess. Word somehow got around that a yankee was visiting the Wellers. A neighboring lad of perhaps ten years of age came in and watched us play for a few minutes. Then he began asking questions.

"Do they really have skyscrapers in America?"

I replied, "Yes, New York City has many skyscrapers that are 75 to 100 stories high."

"Do Americans really have two cars each?"

"Many families have two cars. But some families have no cars at all."

Here my host said: "Son, would you like to do me a favor?"

"Yes sir," responded the youngster.

With a wink at me, my host took a ten-shilling note from his wallet and said: "Would you go the chemist (drug store) and get me a pound of spiders' eyelashes?"

The lad took the note and went off. My host gave a great guffaw.

About 20 minutes later the youngster returned, laid the ten-shilling note on the table, and, without saying a word, departed. The elderly gentleman and I both laughed.

A few days later I was playing chess with the old gentleman again. And again the young fellow came in and observed our play. Then he asked me: "Do they really have cowboys in America?"

"Yes, we have lots of men who work with cattle on ranches," I answered.

"Do they have pistols?"

"No, that's a thing of the past."

My host then interjected: "Son, would you do me a favor?" as he reached for his wallet.

"Well, maybe," the lad cautiously responded.

"Would you take this ten-shilling note to the chemist and get me a pound of moth balls?"

The youngster lit up: "You're not pulling that on me any more.

Moths no more have balls than spiders have eyelashes.''

---

7. AN IRISH WEDDING

An Irish couple, Cassie and Sean, had courted each other for a few years. In their late 20's they wedded in a Catholic church.

After the wedding came the reception, and quite an elaborate affair it was. There was a vast array of foods. Entertainment and funmaking prevailed. But, in accord with the bride's wishes and arrangements, there were no wines, beers, whiskies or alcoholic beverages.

Well into the festivities, the bride espied some men pouring shots of whiskey for each other. Worse, her beloved Sean was amongst the group of tipplers.

Cassie marched straight into the group and berated one and all and then turned to her new mate and said with emphatic finality: "There'll be no drinking in our marriage."

Quite taken aback by this behavior in front of his buddies, Sean just as emphatically shot back with: "I wear the pants in our family. Don't you forget that. I'm a free man. I'll drink whatever and whenever I like." And he downed another jigger of liquor to make his point.

"You'll not touch a drop of this vile stuff ever again," rejoined his wife. With this stinging rebuke, she grabbed Sean's shot glass and threw it to the floor with great force.

In a demonstration of his independence, Sean had several more drinks and became quite inebriated. A friend drove the couple to their new home. Cassie lambasted and chastised Sean even more when they arrived home.

Sean collapsed on a sofa and passed out. Needless to say, there was no consummation that night. The next morning Sean awoke to go to work. He went to their bed where Cassie slept, with the intention of apologizing. Instead he met with a new barrage of castigation and strictures.

He departed the house in indignation with his treatment and went to work. All day he thought about the situation. He felt he had to show his bride that he was the master in their home. So he bought a fifth of whiskey and came home. She took up where she left off, managed to get his bottle and smash it in the sink.

Sean was so upset, he left in a huff and went to a bar where he again became drunk. He was brought home by a friend. Again he slept on a sofa.

For another two weeks the impasse continued. Cassie continued to berate him and lay down the law. Sean not only insisted on his prerogatives to drink but to be the master in his own home.

As this rift continued, both the drinking and chastisements escalated. He missed work and was reprimanded there too. His marriage had not been consummated. He was, in reality, a drunkard.

Cassie realized the hopelessness of the situation and betook herself to the father who had performed the wedding ceremony. As a Catholic she could not walk out on her marriage. She explained the situation to the father.

"I see your problem quite clearly, child. If you want to save this marriage, you must make the home a place of welcome, a place of love, a place he'll treasure more than his senseless pride. Alcohol is an escape from problems he sees as insurmountable. He'll drop his drinking if you become loving and understanding. Above all, don't press the issue."

This made sense to Cassie. She went home and spent the rest of the day making preparations.

Then she awaited the arrival of her unfulfilled husband. She waited and waited and waited.

Well after midnight she heard a noise outside. She opened the door and looked out. There was Sean along a wall trying to put a key into it. She took her drunken husband by the hand, led him inside, and eased him into an easy chair. She put his feet on an ottoman. She lay his head on a soft pillow. She brought him a bowl of warm soup and spoon fed him.

The effect of this attention was obvious. Even in his stupor Sean mumbled his appreciation.

After she fed him, Cassie sat down on the arm of the easy chair and stroked his hair. Sean enjoyed this immensely. Then Cassie whispered into his ear: "Honey, shall we go upstairs and go to bed?"

Sean muttered: "Might as well. When I get home I'm gonna get hell anyway."

8. THERE'S ALWAYS A FIRST TIME!

A Catholic church in New Jersey held a combination fair and carnival as a money-raising event.

Available to the church were the facilities and resources of a full carnival. This included an elephant, a huge animal of about two tons. The church fathers got their heads together and decided to use the elephant in a contest.

The contest would charge entrants a dollar. The winner would take the pot. To win, the contestant had to get the elephant's four feet off the ground all at once.

The contest was an instant success. There was a long line to enter the contest. In a few hours the pot promised to yield the church at least $500 as no one get all the elephant's feet off the ground at once.

Directly, a Jewish lad paid his dollar, picked up a baseball bat and whammed the elephant's genookies. The elephant responded by jumping fully six inches off the ground with all four feet at once. The shocked fathers gave the smart lad the pot.

The fathers got their heads together again. How could they make capital out of this elephant.

They decided upon another contest. Elephants can move their head up and down but, because of straight bones along side their neck to the jaw, cannot move their heads side to side. Contestants would pay a dollar fee to enter and win the pot if they could get the elephant's head to move from side to side.

Again the contest prospered. Again, the pot swelled to over $500. But not a contestant succeeded in getting the elephant's head to move from side to side.

Again, the Jewish lad put in an appearance. Triumphantly, the fathers nudged each other. They were sure they had their nemesis stymied.

The Jewish boy paid a dollar to enter. He went to the pachyderm's monstrous ear and whispered into it: "Mr. Elephant, do you remember what happened to you awhile ago?"

The elephant vigorously moved his head up and down to affirm his memory of the painful experience.

Then the lad whispered: "Mr. Elephant, would you like that to happen to you again?"

And, for the first time in the annals of elephants, one shook its head from side to side.

---

9. THE GREAT GAS WAR

Just before the cartel known as OPEC artificially upped the price of oil by over 300%, there were gas wars among service stations and oil refiners.

In 1972, a major price war took place in New Jersey. The independent stations competed in the price war because their costs were lower. The big chain stations wanted to drive the independents out of business. So they added a new dimension to the struggle.

Big chain stations added customer-attracting devices called contests, lotteries and drawings. They offered big prizes like expensive autos, trips to Europe, TV's, and so on. This caused customers to defect from small independent stations that didn't have the size or clout to print the extensive contest materials, much less match the prizes.

One Jewish gas station operator in New Jersey got a contest

idea. He put a large sign on the highway reading: "Buy gas here. Win secret prize." The word "secret" brought in droves of the curious, and gas sales quickly quadrupled for the operator.

One of the operator's former patrons saw the sign and came in: "Harry, what's with this secret prize?"

"Look Larry, you see that handsome young man in the window? Women who win get to spend an hour with him. You see that lovely lass? Men who win get to spend an hour with her."

"You're not kidding me, are you Harry?"

"No, not at all. It's on the level."

"Fill 'er up," came the order from Larry. He drew for a prize and came up with a nonwinning ticket. So he departed hurriedly.

Within twenty minutes Larry was back in his van and ordered: "Fill 'er up." Again he drew. Again he didn't win.

Larry got a bright idea. He went to K-Mart and bought twelve five-gallon gas cans.

When he came back, Larry filled a can and drew a ticket. Each time, he didn't win. He became more frustrated with each filling and drawing. Finally, he was filling the twelfth can. He made his lucky sign and then drew. For the 14th time he drew a losing ticket.

Exasperated, Larry turned on the station owner: "Harry, I think your damned contest is a fraud!"

"What do you mean my contest is a fraud?" shot back Harry. "You go home and ask your wife. She won twice already!"

---

10. GOING TO HEAVEN

My son, Martin, came to me the other day and said: "Daddy, I had a dream I went to heaven last night."

"You did? What was heaven like?"

"Dad, I was chained to the ugliest girl I've ever seen in my life. She was so ugly, Dad, that I couldn't face her. I wanted to break those chains just to get away from her."

"Dad, you were there too. You were chained to the most beautiful girl I've ever seen. Dad, she was so beautiful, so well-stacked, I wanted to break my chains just to get to her."

"Later, St. Peter came by. I asked him: "St. Peter, what is this? I'm a good Christian. Look what my lot is here. This is supposed to be heaven? And look at my lucky duck Dad over there. He's not even a Christian. How does he rate?"

St. Peter said: "Don't let appearances fool you. You did commit some sins. For your sins, she is your punishment. As for your dad, well, he's her punishment."

---

11. WINNING AN ELECTION

At one time a republican didn't have a chance of winning an election in the State of Oklahoma.

Nevertheless, The Republican Party always put up a candidate for every state and federal office.

On one particular election before the second world war, an enterprising, imaginative, and well-to-do rancher was nominated for the office of U.S. Senator on the Republican Party ticket.

He did some research and found out almost 20% of the voting population was Indian. This much of the vote, plus the usual Republican votes, plus other nonvoters constituted over 70% of the eligible voters.

Our erstwhile rancher decided upon a strategy of appealing to Indian voters as well as Republicans and the indifferent voters.

So, early one September day the Republican Party candidate for U.S. Senator was at an Indian fair on a reservation near Anadarko, Oklahoma. The fair convened with musical fanfare, announcements, speeches and then candidates who made their usual pre-election promises.

When the rancher spoke, he began by saying: "You long-suffering folks have been neglected by our government in Washington. If elected, one of the first things I'll do is see that you get the same rights and privileges enjoyed by the white folks.''

There came a round of clapping and a very vocal ''oola, oola, oola.''

The rancher felt he was making great headway among the Indians. Everything he said met with ever louder clapping and exclamations of ''oola, oola, oola.''

After the speech, because of his reputation, the rancher was invited to be a livestock judge, an invitation he accepted graciously.

The rancher took his judging role very seriously and gave all appearances of being very competent as well.

When he started judging the prize bulls of the Indian 4-H Club members, he tried to appear very thoroughgoing in the case of each giant bull.

By and by he came to a huge bull with its proud Indian attendant conducting him around the animal. As he was going around the rear of the bull, it raised its tail and began copious plops of.......

The Indian attendant cautioned: ''Careful sir not to step in the oola.''

12. POOR ENGLISH

Back in the occupation days in Japan, many Japanese spoke a kind of pidgin English. Many American service personnel tried their best at communication with the Japanese using the same broken English.

On one particular occasion a soldier seasoned in pidgin English approached a lovely Japanese lady and said: ''You, me have tempura, neh?''

The beautiful and demure lady asked: ''You nice man?''

''I be velly nice,'' replied the soldier.

''You come my home? I good cook. Like tempura like you.''

The couple took a train to Shinjuku, a part of Tokyo, continuing to converse in pidgin English.

The soldier felt he was fortunate to meet such a nice Japanese girl.

But, on the way, another American soldier came up and asked the Japanese lady: "Which train do I take to get to Nakano?" To which the companion answered in flawless English: "Sir, you get off in Shinjuku and change to the D train on track seven."

Her surprised companion exclaimed: "You speak such wonderful English. Why didn't you tell me you could speak English so well?"

"Gosh," she said. "I'm happy to hear you speak good English too. English is my native tongue. I'm Hawaiian."

---

13. THE LAST WORD

An atheist and a preacher were arguing about religion. The atheist said accusatively: "You preachers have been promising life after death for 2,000 years. You can't prove you've delivered on a single promise."

The preacher gently responded: "Yes, it is true. We've been bringing God's message of eternal life to the worthy for over 2,000 years. And don't you think it remarkable that we've never received a single complaint of nondelivery?"

"Don't you think it equally remarkable, Reverend, that in all this time neither have you preachers received a single thank-you note?"

---

14. THE IDEAL PLACE TO LIVE

A couple of atheists were attending high school graduation ceremonies for a son and daughter respectively in a West Texas community noted for its colossal Baptist church. The church, with its parking lot, Sunday schools, and rectory occupied a whole city block. In fact, Baptists were the majority of the population.

The atheists were appropriately respectful even though they exchanged derogatory views.

The graduation ceremonies started with the bowing of heads. The Baptist minister gave an invocation that was really a prayer.

"You'd think he'd proselytize for converts in church, not in a high school," observed one atheist to the other.

"Yes, it's disgusting how they try to cram religion down our throats, especially in captive audiences like this."

There came more prayers and laudatory remarks about God, the Lord, and the Savior.

"It's really a travesty that we have to swallow all this religious malarkey," chimed in one atheist.

Another father of a graduating daughter sat next to them. "I couldn't help but overhear what you fellows were saying. I take it that you two are unhappy living among us Baptists?"

"That's to put it mildly," responded one of the atheists. "I've had it up to here with hardshell Baptists," he continued, making a gesture toward his Adam's apple.

The other atheist added. "We'd like to move to an area where there are as few Baptists as there are Moslems here. If I'm not mistaken, there are less than 10% Baptists over in New Mexico. I'm thinking about moving there."

Better yet, there's less than 5% Baptists in Utah," spoke up the other atheist.

The first atheist came back with: "Who wants to put up with the Mormons and their brand of bull?"

"Tell you what fellows," their Baptist neighbor rejoined. "I know a perfect place for both of you to go. There are neither Baptists nor Mormons there."

"Where's that?" asked the atheists in unison.

"Hell!" came their neighbor's curt response.

15. TABLETS OF CLAY

A bishop was visiting a Catholic Parochial school in his See. He went into an eighth grade classroom and began chatting with the students. The teacher was delighted with his visit. Then the bishop began asking questions of the students. He directed one question to a particular student: "Clancy, who broke the tablets upon which were written the Ten Commandments?"

"Sir, I don't know who broke those tablets," responded Clancy. "I sure know that I didn't break them."

The bishop was furious. "Miss McVeigh, how is it that a student of yours doesn't know who broke the tablets?"

"Your holiness," the teacher answered, "Clancy is a very honest boy, and I'm sure he told you the truth. I'm equally sure that no one else in this class broke the tablets either."

The Bishop stormed out and went to the principal's office: "Father," he said, "I asked Clancy who broke the tablets on which were written the Ten Commandments. He said he didn't know who broke them, but that he didn't break them. And Miss McVeigh was sure no one else in her class had broken them. What kind of nonsense do you teach these children here, anyway?"

"Your holiness, I'm sure there's a misunderstanding here. But I don't want to waste your precious time trying to turn up the culprit. Tell me how much those tablets cost and I'll reimburse you."

16. GET YOURSELF A BOARDER

An 86-year old man married an 18-year old girl. Came Monday the oldster, with a long white beard, visited a physician's office.

"Doc, I just got married to a young woman of 18."

"Don't I know it! Your picture's on the front page of today's paper.''

"Doc, I want to have a baby with my new wife. What do you advise?''

"Get yourself a boarder," came the physician's curt answer.

About six months later the elderly gentleman met the physician on the street. He took his hand and started pumping it. "Doc, I'm sure thankful for your advice.''

"Your wife is pregnant?''

"Yup, she sure is!''

"Did you get a boarder?''

"I sure did. And she's pregnant too!''

---

17. GOING TO MIAMI BEACH

A man, Darrell Wells by name, was mandatorily retired from Macy's on his 65th birthday.

Both his pension and social security did not yield enough to support himself and his wife. So he searched for work for two years, but in vain. No one would hire him, and his savings were dwindling.

One day Darrell came home and started packing.

"Darrell, dear, where're you going? Are you leaving me?'' his wife pleadingly asked.

"Honey, I'm going to Miami Beach. The women there are paying $500 a lay.''

His wife, Dorene, also began packing.

"And where do you think you're going?'' demanded hubby.

"Darrell, darling,'' his spouse responded, "I have to come along and take care of you. You'll never make it on $500 a year.''

---

18. WHO IS THE WORLD'S CHESS CHAMPION?

In a certain London chess club, the chess champion of the world offered a reward of 100 pounds sterling to anyone who could beat him. The catch was that those who tried had to pay five pounds to play him. He was never short of challengers, sometimes playing ten or twelve games a day. But he never lost.

One retired well-to-do gentleman came to the club daily, plunked down a five pound note, played the champ, and always lost. This went on for a couple years.

The owner of the club took the chess champ aside one day and said: "Mr. Anderson, our club member, Terence Tarlton, has been playing you every day for over two years. You always beat him. He might soon tire of this and quit. Why don't you drop a game to him to keep it interesting for him? I'll cover the 100 pound award.

So, the following day, Mr. Anderson contrived to lose a game to Mr. Tarlton. To everyone's surprise, Mr. Tarlton never showed up again.

A few months later, the owner met Mr. Tarlton on a street and greeted him: "Mr. Tarlton, why don't we see you at the club anymore?"

"After you've beaten the world champion, who is there left to play?"

---

19. HOW DID YOU COME TO
FATHER FOURTEEN CHILDREN?

"Jeb, how come you and Sandra had 14 children?"
"I guess it's on account of Sandra being hard of hearing."
"What does that have to do with having 14 kids?"
"Well, when we went to bed at night I always asked her if we should go to sleep or what? She always answered 'What?'"

---

20. MISMATCHED SHOES

"Professor, isn't it odd to wear a pair of shoes with one being brown and the other black?"

"What's odder still is that I have another pair at home just like it."

---

21. EXPLAINING FRUSTRATION

"Daddy, what does frustration mean?"

"Better that I show you, son? Get on the extension."

With this the father wrote down a telephone number and then dialed it. When there was an answer he asked: "Is Joe there?"

"Joe doesn't live here," was the response, and the party hung up.

"You see, son, he is annoyed."

A few moments later the father dialed the same number again. "Is Joe there?" he asked.

"Damn it, I told you there's no one here named Joe," the man answered as he slammed down the receiver.

"You see, son, he is mad."

Then for a third time he dialed the same number. When the answer was made, the father said in a changed voice: "This is Joe. Have there been any calls for me?"

From the line came a pause instead of a response. The father hung up: "You see, son, he is now frustrated."

---

22. A WAY TO MAKE DONUTS

A group of proper Boston ladies decided they would like to tour a navy ship which was moored at the docks. A call to the ship elicited an invitation to a formal tour of the ship and its facilities.

The duty of conducting them befell an ensign. He took the ladies through the maze of decks, quarters, and facilities on the huge floating city. At one point, all were in the bakery. A sailor was slapping pieces of dough against his belly button.

One of the ladies asked: "Sir, what is that sailor doing?"

"Oh, he's making cookies. He makes a little decoration on

them with his navel.''

"But, officer, isn't that an odd way to make cookies?''

"Lady, if you think that is odd, you should see him make donuts.''

---

23. GOING TO THE DOCTOR

A lady went to see a physician for the first time in her life, at age 40. She waited long but was finally ushered into the physician's office.

"What's your problem," the physician asked?

"Sir, I'm here for a checkup. I'm concerned about female problems.''

"O.K. Miss Porter, get undressed.''

Miss Porter hesitated, gave the physician a coy smile and said: "Alright doctor, but please, you first.''

---

24. WHY SO GLUM CHUM?

A physician went into the lounge of a hospital. There he saw a friend who appeared rather downcast.

"Why so glum, chum?''

"I just did an appendectomy for a thousand dollars.''

"Cheer up pal! A thousand dollars isn't exactly chicken feed.''

"Yeah, but after I did the operation, I found out my patient was well-heeled. I could've taken out a kidney for $5,000.''

---

25. AN EXTENDED VACATION

Did you hear about the physician who went on vacation and enjoyed it so much he extended it to two months?

When he returned to his practice he was out of business. He'd stayed away so long that his patients had gotten well.

26. GETTING LIFE INSURANCE

A 61-year old widower took unto himself a lovely young bride. He loved his wife very dearly, and she was soon pregnant. So he began taking steps to secure his wife for life. He thus made an application for life insurance for a full million dollars, even though there was an extraordinarily high annual cost.

In due course an insurance agent came to interview him and assess his life expectancy.

"Tell me, Mr. Gibbons, how old was your father when he died?"

"Who said my father was dead? He's eighty-eight and well. He operates a clothing store."

"Well then, at what age did your grandfather die?"

"Who said my grandfather was dead? He's 117 and getting married."

"Getting married? Why should he want to get married at 117?"

"Who said he wanted to get married?"

27. PLEASE PUT YOUR BAGS AWAY

A gentleman was sitting on a passenger train. In his car three bags were in the aisle beside his seat. The conductor appeared and asked him: "Sir, do you mind putting your bags on the overhead rack?"

The passenger merely shrugged his shoulders.

A few minutes later the conductor reappeared: "Sir, I asked you nicely to put your bags on the overhead rack. Will you please do that? If these bags are here when I come back, I'm going to throw them off the train."

Again the passenger merely shrugged his shoulders.

About ten minutes later the conductor came back. The bags were still in the aisle. Without a word he picked them up and threw them off the train.

Returning, he said to the passenger: "Mister, I guess that will teach you a lesson."

Shrugging his shoulders yet again, the passenger responded: "No lesson to me, buddy. Those weren't my bags."

28. OIL MONEY

A couple of Texans with neighboring farms both came into substantial oil money at the same time. They decided to celebrate together. They went to the big city of San Antonio for their fling.

After having had a few nips too many, their eyes were caught by a display of Corvairs, the once-popular, rear-engine cars.

Both drove their new cars to a nearby motel where they continued their drinking party. They both arose and inspected their new purchases towards noon of the next day.

One excitedly called to the other: "Someone stole my engine last night."

"Don't fret pal. I have a spare engine in my trunk."

29. THE SCOTCH HONEYMOON

During the 1920's, most of our populace had never seen an airplane, much less ridden in one.

A Scotch couple, both working people, decided not to expend their meager resources on a honeymoon after their forthcoming marriage. They decided upon an inexpensive civil ceremony and, instead of a honeymoon, the thrilling experience of an airplane ride.

Came the marriage and then a trip to the airfield where pilots would take you for a flight of your choice for a specified sum.

The Scotch groom decided upon a flight of fifteen minutes for $10. Like all frugal Scotch people, he offered the pilot $5 for the ride.

"I wouldn't even crank up the plane for $5.00," the pilot replied.

The Scotchman persisted by offering $6.

The pilot, exasperated by the pettiness, made this offer: "I'll take both of you up for 15 minutes. If I so much as hear a peep out of either of you, you owe me $20. If you're perfectly quiet, your rides are free."

The Scottish couple agreed.

The plane was an open-top two-seater. Two could be strapped individually into the rear seat. That's where our newlyweds were settled in.

The pilot had every intention of collecting $20 for the outing. So he took the couple up and then began some aerial virtuosity. He put the plane in a dive and heard nothing. Then he went into a loop. Still he heard nothing. Then he went into a spin. Still not a peep. Then he flew the plane upside down. The Scotchman was very intent on a free ride. For fifteen minutes the pilot made a terrifying flight of sharp banks, loops and dives. During all these maneuvers, the pilot heard no gasp of terror or fright.

The plane was brought in. A hair-raisingly rough and bouncy landing was made. Still not a whimper. When the plane stopped, the pilot got out to witness a bedraggled and tearful Scotchman.

"I sure have to hand it to you. I didn't heard a peep from either of you."

"I know," said the Scotchman. "But I almost let go when me wife fell out."

30. A SPINSTER MARRIES

A school teacher, who was extraordinarily devoted to her mother, became so wrapped up in her profession that the years slipped by quickly. When she was 40 she realized her ambitions to have a husband, home and family were fast fading. So she abruptly left both mother and teaching. Before she departed, her mother extracted a pledge to "call me every day."

The lovely spinster went to Miami. She made friends and was invited to a party. At the party she was introduced to a middle-aged ship captain who, like her, had devoted himself to his profession with such a passion that he was a bachelor.

Our heroine was so betaken by the charm, wit, and overpowering masculinity of the captain that dates for affairs, outings and parties became an everyday affair. One day she spent aboard his yacht. She met dolphins, sailfish, and many other forms of sea life. Her daily reports to her mother were exciting and glowing.

After three weeks she said to her mother: "Mom, we're getting married next week."

Every day daughter faithfully reported the pre-wedding events and preparations to her mother. Finally she called: "Mom, we were married today," and reported the pomp and pageantry of her wedding to a well-known master of the seas. At the end of the call she said: "Mom, nothing has happened yet."

The next day mom received a call telling her of preparations for a honeymoon at sea aboard the captain's yacht. She closed her remarks again with: "Mom, nothing happened yet."

The third day of her marriage, she wired her mother a terse wire: "We're honeymooning aboard the yacht. Nothing happened yet."

The next day she sent another wire: "Mom, the captain got onto a chest of drawers last night. He humped on me. Mom, I had the most wonderful experience of my life."

The next day the daughter received a wire that read: "Come home quick. Papa just broke both legs."

31. PICKING YOUR HEIRS

A Jewish refugee from Poland came to America in 1940. In Poland he had owned a textile mill making specialty cloths and lines of fine clothing. As he had cached lots of funds abroad, he was able to start a similar operation in America. During the war and in the postwar era, his business thrived, and in the early 1950's, he had over 1,100 employees and was grossing over $30 million annually.

The refugee's life was wrapped up in his business almost entirely. He rarely went to a synagogue or associated with others outside of business transactions.

After 20 years the expatriate businessman came down with a lingering illness. He was 85 and realized he might die. He thought about his situation. He called an attorney to his bedside and made an unusual bequest. As he had no heirs, he immediately transferred all his assets equally to the 1,100 existing employees. He appointed as trustees the three topmost managers or whoever the worker/owners might elect. He stipulated that so long as he might live, his modest needs would be met. He further made a rather odd stipulation. When he died, his trustees were each to deposit $1,000 on his chest at the funeral.

This noble and humanitarian refugee died after a few more months. Came the day of the funeral when thousands of employees, community members and business persons from far and near attended the funeral. Prior to this there was a private service which was attended by an Englishman, a German, and a Dutchman, his appointed trustees and topmost managers.

As the Englishman passed the bier he deposited ten new $100 bills on the chest with "Sorry old chap."

Then came the German, stiff and solemn. He bowed in obeisance and deposited a rare but crisp $1,000 bill.

The Dutchman approached, equally solemn, and deposited his check for $3,000 and took the $2,000 as his change.

---

32. HOW TO PAD AN INVOICE

Over a century ago, mills were operated by belt systems, usually all hooked up to a single power source.

.ile factory had its belt systems stop all at once.
.nd workers were idled. After an hour the in-house
.e personnel couldn't get the mill running. The des-
pe.   .ner sent a man in a horse-drawn buggy to fetch the
factor͵ s designer who lived three miles distant.

Within half an hour the design engineer was greeted by the mill owner: "All our belt systems are down, and I'm paying a thousand people to do nothing. I'll pay you a hefty bonus to get things going in a hurry."

The engineer ran to the main drive system, and in a minute all systems were going.

The owner then asked the engineer: "How much do I owe you?"

One thousand dollars replied the engineer.

"One thousand dollars? Would you give me an itemized invoice on that?"

"Certainly," replied the engineer.

A few moments later the following statement was submitted:
Service call..............$5
Turning screws...........$1
Knowing which screws to turn........$994.00.

---

33. THE ENTERPRISING FRENCH FARMER

A French pig farmer had his acreage cleaved by a new highway. He found himself with lots of highway frontage. He tried to get advertisers, businesses, and institutions to avail themselves of his frontage. No one was interested. He thus undertook to create his own enterprises.

His first enterprise involved using both his frontage and his pigs. He made a pigsty beside the road. Then he put a big sign up to attract motorists: "Win 1,000 francs in ten minutes." The sign hadn't been up for more than ten minutes before an Englishman stopped. He found he had to pay a 50 franc entrance fee and spend

10 minutes on a little platform directly over the pigsty to win the prize money.

The Englishman hadn't been in the pigsty more than two minutes when he emerged muttering. "Wouldn't be bloody worth it for ten times as much," and departed.

Almost immediately a German stopped. He paid the entrance fee. He walked in while the farmer timed him. He was there three minutes, four minutes, then five minutes. The farmer became concerned, thinking that the fellow was overcome by the powerful ammoniated stench. As he started in, the German came out, mouthing obscenities in German.

When the farmer came out, another customer awaited him, a Polock in popular parlance. The Polish fellow paid the entrance fee and went inside. The farmer timed the stay. At five minutes he became concerned. He mused to himself: "Did the contestant pass out? Maybe he's used to working with pigs, and that will cost me a thousand francs." He waited two more minutes and started inside. Imagine his surprise to meet the pigs walking out!

---

34. THE BIGGEST LIAR

At and annual Liar's Club meeting in New York, the club voted the following story the biggest lie of the year award: "I got on a liner to go to Southhampton, England. The first day out I was strolling on the deck with a friend. A powerful wind came up and caused me to fall overboard. Imagine my good fortune when a dolphin not only rescued me, but delivered me to Southampton two days before the ship arrived. I was on the pier to meet my friend and fellow passengers when the ship arrived."

When the award was announced, a man arose and protested: "You can't give this fellow The Liar's Club Award. This gentleman is telling the truth. I am the friend he spoke of. I was there and saw it all happen exactly as he told you."

35. FIRST CHOICE

Two brothers were left their father's estate. They decided to divide up the farm and each take half. But almost immediately they began quarreling over who got what. So bitter was the squabble, they decided to present the matter privately to a probate judge and let his decision be binding.

Within two minutes the judge gave them a binding guideline for dividing up the estate: "Jack, you are older. I want you to divide up the estate. Jerry, I accord you the privilege of choosing your half first."

36. THE POWER OF ADVERTISING

At 34, a delicatessen owner decided it was time to get a wife, a home and start his family. As he had been working from 7:00 A.M. to 11:00 P.M. seven days a week since age 22 when he inherited the deli, he didn't want to go through all the time consuming rigors of romancing one or more women. So he put an ad in the paper beginning with "Wife wanted."

A few days later a customer remarked: "Rubin, I noticed you had an ad in the paper for a wife. Get any answers?"

"Did I get any answers? Look," he said, motioning to three full boxes of letters.

"Gee, lots of women want to be your wife."

"These letters aren't from women. They're from men."

"From men? Why should men write you?"

"They're offering me theirs."

37. HEAVEN'S REWARDS

At Texas A & M one football season, three talented football players came together. Until they graduated four years later, they were to be found together constantly. They all made the first team as seniors, and one even made the All- America team. When they graduated, they all started businesses in College Station so they could be together for life.

One thing they'd never do: They wouldn't miss an Aggie football game no matter where it was played, Tokyo, London or College Station.

About twenty years later three successful businessmen readied themselves for a hundred mile trip to the Texas University Memorial Stadium in Austin. But last minute business delayed one of them to the point that they all had only 90 minutes in which to travel, park and get into the stadium by kickoff time.

"I'll get us there on time," announced Kevin. He drove at speeds of 80 to 100 miles per hour. In 50 minutes they were only about 30 miles away when a long hill of only two lanes was encountered with two-way traffic. No passing of course. Worse, a huge truck pulling two semi-trailers was going upgrade at only 30 miles an hour. After riding behind for half a minute, one of the trio urged: "Kevin, get around this truck or we'll be late."

Kevin pulled out from behind the truck for a look only to be struck by another huge freight truck barreling downgrade at about seventy miles per hour.

That very afternoon, St. Peter greeted three new entrants to heaven. To the first, he said: "I see you've led an exemplary life. You never cheated on your wife. You never cheated in business. And you gave generously to help the less fortunate. I'm going to give you a Rolls Royce to get around in."

To the next, St. Peter intoned: You cheated on your wife when the opportunity arose. You did the same in business. And you gave very little to charity. I'm awarding you a motorcycle to get around on."

To the third, St. Peter was harsh: "I don't know what you're doing here. You cheated on your wife, even neglecting your family. You cheated in business. You even cheated your two friends here. And you never helped the poor. I'm awarding you a bicycle to get around on."

Despite the disparity, the three remained fast friends in heaven.

One day, after many years, two of the friends came upon their friend with the Rolls Royce yelling and screaming in a rage. He was pounding on the hood, pulling his hair and stomping.

"Brother, there's no call for this. We're in heaven. We got it made. Why are you so upset?"

"My wife just made it. And she's on roller skates."

---

38. MYSTERY OF THE BEARDLESS LINCOLN PENNIES

In the 1950's, the U.S. Department of the Treasury had one of the oddest cases in its history. Perfectly minted pennies were showing up with Lincoln beardless!

A team of T-Men were put on the case and began tracing their source. A small West Texas town where I lived was pinpointed. Several stores were put under watch with their owners and cashiers alerted.

One day my father and I went shopping for a few items. My father began haggling over prices and asked for price reductions on almost every item as was his practice. Then he would pay the clerk slowly, usually with pennies collected from a couple dozen gumball and trinket machines he owned and serviced.

In the middle of paying his tobacco and grocery bill, my father was arrested for passing counterfeit pennies. When they searched him he had well over a hundred pennies, everyone of which bore a beard on Lincoln! My father was released. But, nevertheless, the beardless pennies continued to show up from our little town.

Again the T-men came to town. Again they pinpointed and arrested my father. Again his pocket had only perfect pennies with beards. Again he was released.

A thoughtful and observant agent did a study and made a report that characterized my father as a terrible penny pincher, so much so that, in the spending process, he held onto his money so tightly, the beards on Lincoln pennies came off!

---
39. SMALL TOWN DOCTOR RETIRES

A late-marrying physician in a small town became a father when he was fifty. He doted on his son and gave him every advantage. He wanted his son to be a medical doctor. So he groomed him for that profession. He wanted his son to take over his practice.

When he was in his late seventies, he was rewarded. His son completed internship and came home to take over his father's practice. The transition was soon made. The old doctor received glowing reports about how wonderful his son was. So he set off for a six month trip around the world with lots of sight-seeing stops.

When he returned he found his son struggling to make ends meet in the small town. So father visited his son to discuss the situation.

"How is Mrs. Puckett, son?"

"Dad, I got here well over five months ago."

"How is Brother South and his wife?"

"Their problems were simple, dad. Both have been well almost six months."

"And how about Mrs. Mason?"

"Dad, her case was a snap. She's been well for months."

Son and father reviewed a number of other cases. All were no longer clients because the son had guided them to wellness.

Then the father reprimanded his son! "Son, these are the people who formed the backbone of my practice for the last twenty to fifty years. Their patronage supported us through the years. Their patronage built this house. Their patronage sent you through medical school and paid your training bills. So you come home and, like an idiot, get them all well."

40. THE TRAVELING SALESMAN

An industrial salesman traveled from city to city, staying two or three days in each while he called on clients.

When he came home on weekends, his wife told him how much she missed him. Gradually she voiced suspicions, and then became jealous. She accused him of infidelity. Her husband protested his innocence and invited her to share his travels, an offer she accepted.

The salesman made advance deals for hotel rooms at a package price. He ate his meals willy nilly during the days and evenings wherever he was. He rarely ate expensive hotel fare.

At one hotel he made a deal of three nights for just $100 for himself and his wife. She stayed in the hotel room while he made his business calls. In the evenings he took his wife out for dinner and entertainment.

When he checked out the desk manager presented him a bill for $160.

"What's this $60 about?" he demanded. "I made a deal when I came--three nights for a hundred bucks."

"Oh, that $60 isn't for your room. It's for food."

"Food? We didn't eat any of your food!"

"Too bad, it was there for you."

Getting a bright idea the salesman pulled out a hundred dollar bill. "Here's a hundred for the room. I'm charging you $60 for going to bed with my wife."

"But I didn't touch your wife!"

"Too bad! She was there for you."

41. THE CONSUMMATION

A working couple got married. They did not plan a honeymoon as both had to be at work every working day. The reception and partying on Sunday evening kept them up so long that they didn't get to bed until 2:00 A.M. Both were tired and both had to get up at 6:00 A.M. Even so he made an approach but was gently rebuffed because of lateness. So there was no consummation that night.

That afternoon, husband and wife arrived home from work at about the same time. She began making their new apartment shipshape, sent him on sundry errands, and enlisted his help for several tasks. With a sleep deficit, he went to bed at 11:00 P.M. He roused with certain impulses at 2:00 P.M. when his wife came to bed. Again, she put him off with "I'm too tired." So there was no consummation that night either.

On Tuesday, both arrived home and continued fixing up. Both retired early. This time she disappointed him with: "My period came today." So, for a third night, there was no consummation.

On Wednesday, he checked his wife's condition. She informed him her period was still on. Thusly, there was no consummation on the fourth day.

On the fifth day he again made an approach. He was parried with: "My period is still on."

On the sixth day he tried again. She said: "Honey, there is still some flow."

On the seventh day, a Saturday, they each had off all day. In the midafternoon both took a rest on the bed. He made an approach which he was sure would be, at last, the consummation.

His wife put him off with: "What's the matter with you, honey? You just want it every day?"

---

42. THE CAPTAIN'S SECRET

In the helm room of the ship he commanded, the captain kept a drawer perpetually locked. No one was allowed in his presence when he opened it. Naturally, the contents of the locked drawer aroused curiosity of the ship's crew.

The mystery of the drawer's contents was a secret for 23 years until the captain died. The first thing the first mate and other officers did was to take the captain's keys, rush up to the helm room, and open up the drawer.

Upon opening the drawer, they found it empty except for a cross with arrows at four ends marked <u>forward, stern, lee</u> and <u>port.</u>

---
43. REASONS FOR TAKING LEAVE

A sailor in the U.S. Navy went before his commanding officer and requested leave.

"Sailor, why do you wish to take leave at this time. You know we're scheduled to go to sea within three weeks? "

"Well, sir, my wife is pregnant and due any day. I don't want to leave her that way."

"Sailor, I'm granting you two weeks leave immediately. Next!"

Another sailor stepped up and requested a two-week leave.

"Sailor, why do you wish to take a two-week leave. We're due to go to sea in three weeks."

"Sir, my wife is not pregnant. I don't want to leave her that way."

---
44. APPLYING FOR A FURLOUGH

A soldier went before the captain of his company to request a leave.

"Corporal, why do you wish to go on a furlough?"

"Sir, I have a wife and four children. She just called me for help because two of the kids are sick."

"That's very odd, soldier. I received a call last week from your wife. She asked me for a raise in her dependency allowance. Further, she asked me to keep you on base. She said you were always drinking at home, beating her up, slapping the children, and being abusive. I must deny your request.''

The soldier turned to go. Then he turned to the captain. ''Forgive me sir, but I want to set the record straight. I have no children and I've never been married.

---

45. GOING TO A CATHOLIC UNIVERSITY

A Jewish high school graduate announced to his father: ''Papa, I want to go to Fordham University in the Bronx.''

''Son, you know we're Jewish. You really mean Yeshiva University in the Bronx, don't you?''

''No, papa, I mean Fordham.''

''A Jew has no call to go to a Catholic institution. The first thing, you know, you'll be telling me you want to marry a Catholic.''

''Papa, I've made up my mind. I want to go to Fordham.''

''Son, if you've made up your mind, I won't interfere.''

A year and a half after entering Fordham, the son went before his father to make a request. He was greeted with: ''Don't tell me. You want to marry a Catholic.''

Yes, papa, I want to marry a Catholic.''

''Son, what are you going to do when your wife calls you a damned dirty Jew?''

''Oh, dad, we've been through that already. I just called her a stinking nigger.''

---

46. A JEW IN A CATHOLIC UNIVERSITY

A Jewish student was attending Fordham University. He made friends with several Catholics. He became very close to one of his friends, an Italian of whom he was especially fond because he studied quite hard, was a knowledgeable and charming conversationalist, and exhibited lots of ambition. So, one day, he asked some questions of his close friend.

"Guido, why do you study so hard? What do you hope to be?"
"Confidentially, Dave, I hope someday to be a bishop."
"With your talent, is that all you want to be?"
"You mean I should try to be a cardinal?"
"Only a cardinal? Surely you can do better than that."
"Don't tell me I could be a pope?"
"Be only a pope? Why not try for the very top? One of our boys made it."

47. VIVA LA DIFFERENCE!

A man had occasional tiffs with his wife. News of these run-ins got to a nudist friend.

"Why don't you and Wilma become members of the nudist colony? It'll work wonders for your relationship."

"And why should we join a nudist colony?"

"It's a wonderful way to air your differences."

48. CELEBRATING SUCCESS

George Bernard Shaw wrote a fabulously successful play based on a Greek fable wherein a statue of a beautiful woman comes to life. Shaw's version of Pygmalion rescued a lovely but crude, unlettered woman from the streets and transformed her into a beautiful and charming woman of culture, except in a few areas. This play became even more widely known as the movie, *My Fair Lady*.

When Pygmalion premiered in London, it was an instant success. A celebration party was held immediately after the first performance.

At the party the beautiful actress who played the lead role of Pygmalion is reputed to have said to Shaw: "We should have a baby. With your brains and my looks, it would be a smashing genius!"

Shaw is reputed to have replied: "I prithee my lovely lady to think what our child would be like if it had my looks and your brains."

49. MY SON, THE ACCOUNTANT

A certain clothier in the Midwest had been in business for more than 30 years and was regarded as a solid citizen.

He had a son who graduated from the local schools and went on to Ohio State University where he studied business and accounting. He graduated and underwent extra training in accounting.

When he came home he qualified as a CPA. His first client was, of course, his father who had supported him through the years.

One of his first steps was to do something his father had never done: make and evaluate the inventory; tabulate payables and receivables; depreciate fixtures and list assets at current market value.

When a statement was finally made, the son said: "Father, I hate to be the bearer of bad news, but your liabilities are greater than your assets. You're bankrupt. You should close your doors."

"Son, business is better than ever for me. Your mother and I have lived well on this business for 33 years. From its earnings we built our home. It clothed us and you. It put you through school. It put you through college. Your training costs came out of this business. It paid for the fine cars we've had. Did I have to spend all that money putting you through college to be told I'm bankrupt and should close down?"

50. FOLLOWING BUSINESS TRENDS

A father operated a fabulously successful truck stop on a very busy highway where gas and diesel fuel, many sundry auto and truck needs, and consumer items were sold. He also operated a restaurant.

He had a son in whom he took great pride. When he sent him to college, he made sure it was the best business school that would admit him. His son graduated from the school with high honors.

When he came home, his father put him to work in the family business. The son, with all his business training, kept an eye on operations and, as well, the general business climate. One day he informed his father: ''Papa, a serious business recession is near. Many businesses will fail. Trucking will go way down. We should cut our expenses drastically. You're spending over 15% of your gross on advertising alone. We don't need all those billboards and newspaper spreads. Even in good times you shouldn't spend more than 5% of gross on advertising. In view of the forthcoming drop in business, we should cut our advertising outlays to the bone.''

The father cancelled all his contracts with the billboard company. He cut all expenses. And sure enough, his business went down. In fact, it went down by over 50%. And, indeed, there was a recession. He commented to a business friend: ''My son is a business genius. He saw all this coming months ago. If I hadn't cut expenses as I did, I'd be in a terrible mess now.''

51. THE JEALOUS WIFE

A businessman hired a beautiful secretary. Soon, his wife became jealous of her. And it was not long before she was charging him with adultery. If he was the slightest bit late or both were out of the office at the same time, she accused him. During the day, she became a pest with her checkup calls.

The jealous wife became progressively more morbid and unbearable. By this time his secretary was well aware of the situation. "Look, George," she said, "if your wife is going to believe we're having an affair, shouldn't you, at the very least, get the benefit of it?"

This looked reasonable to George. So he accepted her invitation to spend a couple hours with her. He took her to her apartment after work one day and spent two delightful hours with her. As he was preparing to leave, his secretary said, "Let me fix you up for going home. When you get home, tell your wife the truth exactly as it has happened up to this point." Then she rubbed some blue powder on his fingers and thumbs and sprinkled some on his white cuffs and shirt waist.

When he arrived home, his wife immediately laced into him with: "You've been out with Gloria again. I called the office, and both of you left together. Admit it, George. You can't lie to me anymore."

"Yes, darling, I was out with Gloria. She took me to her apartment. I ravished her twice. My joy was great, simply indescribable."

Taken aback, his wife surveyed him with a glower: "You're a terrible liar, George! You've been out shooting pool with the boys again."

---

52. SAVING A FORTUNE

A salesman called on a lady in her home. He offered her a vacuum cleaner. Right off the top he offered: "I can save you $350 on this $700 cleaner. The price is right."

The lady knew she had a great savings opportunity, but she demurred: "Look, I need a vacuum cleaner. I sure want yours. But we saved $12,000 by buying this house at auction. We bought bedding and furniture at a savings of over $5,000. Last week we saved over $400 on a washer and dryer. The other day we saved $350 on a new refrigerator. I'm sorry, but we can't afford to save anymore."

53. THE DYING JEW

A physician told a Jewish client he had only a few weeks to live. He became progressively worse. Matters came to a point that he said to his wife: "Sarah, I'm dying. Get me a priest."

"Darling, you mean I should get a rabbi, don't you?"

"No, get me a priest."

"But, Sol, we're Jewish. Why should you want a priest?"

"Honey, I'm years behind on my pledge at the synagogue. And the Catholics are wonderful. They have a go now, pay-later plan."

54. HOW TO EAT FOR FREE

A couple of salesmen were hungry and searched for a place to eat. They decided to eat sandwiches at a diner.

"Your turn for the tab, Buddy," reminded one as they sat down at a table.

"O.K., it's my turn. Betcha a buck our lunch won't cost me a cent."

"You're on!"

The treating salesman ordered two tuna fish sandwiches when the waiter arrived. When the sandwiches were brought, the waiter was greeted with: "Could we exchange these tuna fish sandwiches for two turkey sandwiches?"

"Of course." The waiter took the tuna fish sandwiches away and brought two turkey sandwiches in their stead.

The salesmen enjoyed their repast. Then the waiter presented the bill for the two turkey sandwiches. "Waiter, there must be a mistake here. You're billing us for two turkey sandwiches. Didn't we trade you two tuna fish sandwiches for the turkey sandwiches?"

"Yes, you did, but you didn't pay for the tuna fish sandwiches."

"Why should I pay you for the tuna fish sandwiches? We didn't eat them," said the salesman as they departed a flabbergasted waiter.

55. TERMINATING AN ACQUAINTANCE

Beautiful Betty to her arriving friend: "Eleanor, I just met a most wonderful guy, the one standing over there. He was warm and friendly. He was inviting me out to dinner. Then he just froze up on me and walked away. Can you imagine that?"

Eleanor: "Perhaps he spotted me. That's my hubby."

56. HOW TO EAT MORE

It's not necessary to be a glutton to eat more!

If you eat less, you'll live longer. And the longer you live, the more you'll eat.

57. THE BETTING CAPTAIN

An army officer was widely known in the service as "The Betting Captain." He seemed to bet on just about everything with just about anybody and usually won.

At a post in New Jersey he made a bet with the commanding general. He won the bet, embarrassing the general before other officers. It was no surprise, therefore, when, a few days later, the captain was transferred to a remote post in Alaska.

The day of his arrival at his new station, he was invited to eat at the commanding general's table with other officers. As they were finishing their meal, he looked at the general with alarm and said with much concern: "Sir, you have TB!"

"Captain, I just had a physical. I got a clean bill of health. I can't take you seriously."

"But sir, you know I was in the Medical Corps during the war. I've had a lot of experience with tuberculars. You have TB, and I swear it."

"I'm in excellent health, Captain. You can't be serious."

"Sir, I'm dead serious. I'm so sure of it that I'll bet you a hundred dollars that you have TB."

The general was visibly shaken. If the betting captain who had a reputation for winning his bets would wager a hundred dollars, there might be something to it. So he parried with: "Captain, I accept your bet. How do you propose to prove I have TB?"

"During the war, sir, we had a field test. We inserted a white candle up the rectum. In TB cases, the candle came out blood tinged."

The general agreed to the test. They went to the general's quarters where the test was made. The candle came out as white and as clean as when inserted. The captain appeared crestfallen. Without saying a word, he gave the general a hundred dollars.

The general dressed and embraced the captain: "Don't take this too badly, captain. I know your reputation for winning your bets."

As soon as the captain was gone, the general phoned the commanding general of the captain's last post: Triumphantly, he said, "I just won a hundred dollars from the betting captain!"

"You did? How did you manage that?"

The Alaskan general related the events.

"You moron," stormed the general in New Jersey. "Before he left here he bet me $1,000 he'd have a candlestick up your ass within 24 hours after arriving."

---

58. INCOME AND OUTGO

If your outgo is greater than your income, your upkeep will be your downfall.

59. THE BIG BONFIRE

A small town chamber of commerce held a meeting of its twenty odd merchants. They were presented with some incredible facts that mail carriers were delivering merchandise to their area from only three mail order companies of greater value than all the stores' combined sales for the same goods.

A plan was hatched to destroy the mail order businesses. Through letters to every resident in their trade area, ads in the local paper, and posters, everyone learned the merchants would pay $3.00 for each and every mail order catalog of these three companies they surrendered. A huge bonfire would be held on Saturday celebrating the event.

That Saturday evening over 5,000 catalogs were collected in a huge pile from the trade area's 2,000 households. Then a huge bonfire and celebration was held at which the catalogs were soaked in gasoline and torched.

The following Monday the postmaster let the word out that the effort was a failure. The Post Office handled thousands of postcards and letters that day addressed to the three mail order companies asking for another catalog.

60. LIFE AFTER DEATH

"Alice, do you believe in life after death?" asked her employer.

"Yes sir, I really do. Why do you ask?"

"Yesterday I let you off to attend your grandmother's funeral. In the afternoon she stopped by to pick you up a bit early for a shopping trip."

61. HOW DO YOU PRONOUNCE HAWAII?

Two passengers on a plane to Hawaii became embroiled as to

the state's pronunciation.

"It's pronounced Ha-va-ee," stubbornly maintained one.

Equally adamant, the other insisted it was pronounced Hah-wah-ee.

Each wagered $50 they were right.

"How do we determine the winner? "

"Let's ask the first person we see on landing."

"Okay!"

Upon landing, the couple accosted a man sporting colorful Hawaiian attire.

"How do you pronounce the name of this state?"

"Ha-va-ee, of course."

A shocked mainlander paid $50 to his contender. Then he turned to the apparent Hawaiian and asked: "Tell me, how long have you been in Hawaii?"

"Three veeks."

---

62. GETTING A BATH IN IRELAND

In 1950 I arrived by boat in Dublin from Liverpool. I was cleared by customs. I got into a cab and asked him to take me to a good hotel.

I was dropped off at a hotel. I noted a gratuity passing between the cab driver and the hotel person on duty.

I had not been in the hotel long before I discovered it had no bath. The sink in one corner beside a flush toilet had only cold running water. I had to shave using cold water.

The next day I went in search of a hotel with a bath. I was visiting the 11th hotel when they answered, "Yes, we have a bath." So I packed up and moved in. My room had a bathroom with a bath tub. Imagine my surprise when I found there was no hot water.

The hotel served meals on a room-and-board basis. At the next meal, I asked my neighbor how one took a bath without hot water?

"The tourists all use the public bath house about five blocks away."

I got directions to the bath house only to find a sign announcing it would open in May. So I returned to my hotel.

That evening I sat next to the same gentleman. He inquired, "Did you get your bath?"

"No, the bath house was closed and won't open for four more months."

Another voice chimed in: "Why should you get a bath, yankee? Only dirty people have to bathe."

62. THE WISDOM OF LINCOLN

Abraham Lincoln had many illustrative stories and jokes in his repertoire. He had one for every occasion.

When he became president, he was besieged by office seekers. Upon taking office, the tide of would-be appointees to office did not lessen. One morning he was told by his secretary, a male to be sure, that about 20 office seekers were outside seeking an appointment to see him.

Instead of taking them one-by-one, Lincoln went out to the waiting room.

All arose in deference to President Lincoln.

"Be seated gentlemen," Lincoln bade them. Then Lincoln launched into a story.

"Once there was a king in England who was fond of fox-hunting. One particularly sunny day, he and his entourage were about to enter a forest. They met a farmer riding his ass. When the farmer learned the king was about to enter the forest to hunt fox, he advised the king, 'Your highness, I advise you not to go into the forest today. There'll be a deluge, and your party will get soaked to the skin.' And the king said, 'My weather forecaster has predicted a fair and sunny day. We're going in.'

"The party went into the forest. It clouded up and a rainstorm soon ensued. The hunt was terminated and the party, soaked and shivering from cold, rode back to the castle. Immediately upon arriving back, the king sent for the farmer they had met.

"When the farmer was ushered into the king's presence, the king said: 'I'd like to engage you as the court weather forecaster.' Whereupon the farmer confessed, 'Your majesty, it's not me that knows the weather. It's my ass.' Well, then, I want to hire your ass as the court weather forecaster.'

"The ass was hired. The king was happy to have a reliable weather forecaster, but vowed that was the worst appointment he ever made to his court."

After a pause, one of the listeners impatiently asked President Lincoln: "Why did he king say that was the worst appointment he'd ever made?"

"Because," Lincoln retorted, "after that appointment, the king was pestered by every ass in the land seeking an appointment to his court."

63. MOSQUITO STORY

In a certain, open-air cafe on a sidewalk in New York City, one summer, the mosquitoes bothered the customers quite a bit. On one particular evening, a voice was heard to say: "Damn these New York mosquitoes. They're the worst bloodsuckers I've ever seen."

A voice drawled: "You think these are mosquitoes? Our skeeters are so big in Texas, just one can take all the blood outta ya."

"Those mosquitoes are midgets, chimed in another voice. One of our mosquitoes landed in Elmendorf Air Force Base in Alaska, and a refueling crew put 50 gallons of gasoline into it before they discovered their mistake."

64. THE MINISTER'S TREAT

A Baptist minister took a vacation from his home in Indiana to Wyoming. So low were his finances that he rode on the new Amtrak train rather than on a plane.

The minister returned in two weeks like most--out of funds. He gave his last change as a tip to the porter. While he was standing at the baggage claim area, a beggar came to him: "Spare a dime for a cup of coffee?"

"Why, my good man, I can do better than that," responded the minister. "I'll treat you to a meal."

So the two repaired to the station restaurant and ate sumptuous meals. The minister learned about the rigors of life as a beggar, and the bum learned about the goodness of the lord. But, when it came time to pay, the minister was embarrassed. He had no money. The beggar came up with some bills and paid the tab.

"My good man, I am very sorry. I didn't mean it this way at all. Come, let's take a taxi to my house and I'll reimburse you."

"Nothing doing mister," the bum retorted. "I let you beat me out of dinner, but I'm not going to let you beat me out of a taxi fare too."

65. I'M SORRY I WON THE RACE

When two of my sons became nine and ten years old, I decided, on the occasion of my oldest son's birthday, that they should learn about the birds and the bees. So I told them about reproduction as it really was; how, when hundreds of millions of sperm are ejaculated into the vaginal cavity, they begin a race for the ovum.

"Just think, both of you won that race with the odds hundreds of millions against you."

The very next day was my birthday, a fine New Jersey summer day. I received birthday presents from my wife and children. Later I asked for a very special birthday gift from my oldest son,

David: "Son, would you mow the lawn for me?"

Two hours later the lawn hadn't been touched. I approached my son: "David, you haven't mowed the lawn yet. Is something wrong?"

"Dad, I wish I hadn't won that race."

---

66. BIG BOY!

When my son, Martin, was three, he still wetted the bed. So it fell to Daddy's lot to get him out of bed about three every morning and take him to the toilet. I usually had to coax him for five to ten minutes to get him to do his "wee wee."

When Martin produced, I always patted him on the back and congratulated him with "big boy!"

One morning after he had performed and I praised him with "big boy," I stepped up and began voiding.

Imagine my surprise when my leg was patted and a sweet little voice said "big boy!"

---

67. I'D RATHER DIE HAPPY

When I worked in a business in New York City, my partner and I had from 50 to 70 employees. Our shipping room foreman was a black man who often nipped at the bottle. He was a lovable man and produced excellent results with his crew despite his perpetual alcoholic breath.

One day Willie's wife called: "They took Willie to the hospital for an operation."

Two month's later Willie returned to his job which an assistant had assumed. He had a section of his intestines removed because alcohol had ruined it. He was on a bland diet and warned never to touch alcohol again lest he die.

Willie worked soberly for about two months and then, one morning, my partner and I were told his breath reeked of liquor.

So we sent for Willie.

Willie came up to our sixth floor office and my partner, an M.D. in Europe before he fled to America, let Willie know that we wanted him around a long time and that he was committing suicide. We were surprised when we received his response.

"Look, Docs, it's like this. When I is not drinking I is miserable. When I is drinking, I is happy. I's rather die happy than lives miserable."

---

68. RABBIT FOOD

Meat-Eater to Vegetarian: "It's no, thank you' to your rabbit food."

Vegetarian's Response: "I much prefer rabbit food to buzzard food."

---

69. $10,000 HORSE

A horse farmer received a visitor, obviously a city slicker.

The visitor spotted a nice horse, looked it over and asked: "How much you want for this horse?"

"$10,000," replied the farmer.

"I'll give you $1,000."

"Sold," the farmer said.

The transaction was completed. Then the visitor asked: "Why did you ask $10,000 for this horse when you wanted only $1,000?"

"Thought you might want a $10,000 horse."

---

70. HOW MANY LEGS HATH A SHEEP?

Abraham Lincoln was one of the wittiest presidents ever to grace the White House. One of his favorite ways of dealing with people who assumed too much was this:

"How many legs would a sheep have if you counted the tail as a leg?"

Invariably the answer was "five."

"No," Lincoln would say. "It still has only four legs. Counting the tail as a leg doesn't make it one."

71. THE VALUE OF A HIGH SCHOOL EDUCATION

A high school dropout in a large city applied to a neighborhood bank to fill an opening as a cashier. He took the tests and passed all with flying colors. The final step before being engaged was an interview with the bank president.

The president looked over the application and informed the young man: "I have 11 applications for this position, Robert. I'd rather hire you than any of the rest because you did better on the tests and reflect a better job aptitude than the others. But I can't hire you because you do not have a high school diploma."

Robert could not get other available jobs for the same reason. Thus he responded to a sign in the window of a stationery and gift shop for an errand boy. The elderly gentleman readily hired him at a minimum wage to keep the shop in order, to keep the premises clean, to stock the shelves, to make occasional pickups and deliveries, to make bank deposits, and wait on customers when there were more customers than the owner could deal with.

Within a month, Robert had transformed the shop into a neat and inviting store. Business went up appreciably. The owner doubled Robert's pay.

Within a few months, the elderly gentleman would take off an extra day here and there, leaving Robert in charge. The business continued to thrive upwardly.

Another gift shop in another part of the city went up for sale. In behalf of his employer, Robert looked into the situation and found the location and trade area excellent, but a poorly managed shop. The housewife who operated the store could give but little time to it.

On his recommendation Robert made a very easy deal for the distressed shop for the elderly gentleman. In short order, this stationery and gift shop thrived too.

The elderly gentleman fell ill, and Robert engaged help and operated both shops. The elderly owner became worse and sold his prosperous shops to Robert on very favorable terms: a very small down payment and rather small monthly payments.

Under Robert's management, both stores started earning so much that he soon opened up yet another shop in another part of the city. This store thrived as well. Even before he was 21, Robert was already a successful business man. He kept his accounts in the same neighborhood bank where he had been turned down as a cashier.

In a few years Robert owned eight similar shops in the city and became quite well-to-do. He had mastered the success formula.

One day, on visiting his bank, the president invited him to his office. Robert accepted the invitation. The president greeted Robert cordially and reviewed his meteoric rise in the business world. He congratulated him on his enormous success. Then he banker commented: "Robert, you've been sensationally successful. Your accounts in this bank total more than a million dollars. Tell me, son, where do you think you'd be if you had just completed your high school education?"

"Sir, if I had a high school education, I'd be a cashier in this bank."

72. THE ONE DOLLAR LOAN

A well-dressed man went into a bank and asked for a loan application form. He was directed to a bank officer who routinely gave the gentleman a loan application form and asked him to fill it out.

When the officer got the completed form back, he was taken

aback by a loan application for only one dollar. Thinking that the loan applicant was a practical joker despite its orderliness and correctness, he examined the application cautiously.

The bank executive then asked the applicant for additional references. These were readily supplied. Then the officer haughtily asked: "What kind of collateral can you give us to secure this loan?"

The loan officer was overwhelmed when the applicant handed over stocks and bonds totaling over a million dollars in value. Flabbergasted, the loan officer filled out a receipt for the collateral and drew a cashier's check for one dollar payable to the applicant.

At the end of one year, the gentleman returned to the bank and told the loan officer he'd like to renew his loan. Nonplussed, the loan officer accepted 10c as interest and renewed the loan.

A year later the same gentleman asked yet again to renew the loan. Not wanting to be embarrassed the bank officer again accepted the 10c interest payment and renewed the loan.

When the transaction was completed, curiosity overtook the loan officer: "Tell me sir, why do you keep renewing a loan for only a dollar?"

The gentleman replied with a question: "Can you tell me any place else where I can keep my valuables in safekeeping for just 10c a year?"

73. WHAT WERE YOU STEALING?

During the Second World War, there was a German civilian who worked in a prisoner-of-war camp. One afternoon the worker came to the back gate pushing a wheelbarrow of carpenter's scrap. The brawny guard eyed the worker suspiciously and said: "Hans, what have we here?"

Hans replied: "Building wastes for disposal." Nevertheless, the guard poked through the contents and confirmed the declaration.

The following day Hans again came with a wheelbarrow of refuse, this time a load of old rags. Again the wary guard inspected the contents carefully and passed Hans through.

The next workday, the scene repeated; only this time the wheelbarrow was loaded with discarded newspapers. The ever suspicious guard not only looked through the load, but tapped the handles and peered under the barrow lest Hans was concealing something. Finding nothing, he passed Hans through one more time.

The following week Hans came with a wheelbarrow of dirt and gravel. "Aha," the guard thought, "He's been setting me up. He's probably stealing something in this load."

So the guard had Hans turn the entire load over and spread the dirt and gravel over the pavement. Only dirt and gravel were to be seen. Poor Hans laboriously recovered the dirt and gravel and reloaded the wheelbarrow.

Almost everyday Hans came through the gate with a wheelbarrow of refuse and wastes. The suspicious guard never found anything.

By and by, the war ended. Everyone was discharged and the camp dismantled.

A few months after the war the demobilized guard spotted Hans on the street. He laid a heavy hand on Hans' shoulder and demanded: "Hans, the war is over. I knew you were stealing something from the camp. Now that it makes no difference, please tell me what you were taking."

"Dumkopf, you saw it with your own eyes. I was stealing wheelbarrows."

74. A GOOD GOING BUSINESS

A wealthy banker divorced his wife just short of their 50th wedding anniversary. Friends and associates were appalled.

They were even more appalled when, two months later, he married a beautiful 20-year-old cashier of his bank.

He lavished his new wife with expensive gifts and an expensive car. He bought a luxurious home in an exclusive neighborhood.

After a few months of marriage, a vice-president of his bank had a little conference with him. "Sir, I think you should know that your new wife spends twice as much time with other men as she does with you."

"I know that," said the rich banker. "But I'd rather have one third of a good going business than 100% of a bankrupt business."

75. I WANT TO MEET A SUPER RICH MAN!

A stunningly beautiful model and cover girl in New York City let her booking agent, a famous socialite, know that she would like to meet a super rich man.

A few days later the model was invited to a penthouse party where she was assured by her hostess she would meet a super rich man.

At the party her hostess introduced her to a handsome, well-dressed, well-mannered and modest Texan.

About an hour later the model reproached her hostess: "You said you were going to introduce me to a super rich man. That Texan has a spread of only 102 acres."

"Yes, honey," rejoined her hostess. "Didn't he tell you his 102 acre spread is practically all of downtown Houston?"

76. ARE GO-GO GIRLS LIKE DOLLS?

A young lad came into the house and asked his mother: "Mama, do go-go girls come apart like dolls?"

"No, son. Why do you ask?"

"That's funny. Daddy just told that man in the yard he screwed the ass off a go-go girl last night.

---
77. THE WORLD'S GREATEST VIOLINIST

A world renown violinist, Gischa Gaifetz, often boasted that his playing could charm the breasts of savage beasts.

One day, a wealthy New York City businessman challenged him, wagering $25,000 that Gischa could not charm the breasts of savage beasts.

Gischa accepted the challenge. They agreed to go to the African jungle to make the test.

So Gischa flew to Africa with his Strad and the businessman in a chartered jet. They hired a safari to take them into the jungle. They trekked into the jungle and came upon a clearing which they decided was an appropriate place. Gischa began playing the most captivating tunes on his Strad. Presently, birds fluttered down and formed a circle around him. Then came zebras, monkeys, chimps, wildebeests, flamingos, wild dogs, and scores of other animals to join in the circle, all rapt.

Gischa Gaifetz was on the verge of declaring himself the winner when a giant lion bounded through the circle, grabbed Gischa, ripped him apart, and began devouring him.

The entranced animals were stunned. The zebra asked: "Mr. Lion, why did you kill him?"

The lion responded: "Eh, what did you say?"

---
78. A LITTLE KNOWN GREAT VIOLINIST

A world famous conductor, Maestro Arthuro Toscanini, had one of the world's finest orchestras in New York City. Toscanini's first violinist was truly great. He had played under Toscanini for over 20 years, even when Toscanini was a relatively unknown Italian conductor.

Toscanini was well aware of his first violinist's enormous talent but was annoyed by Luigi's constant face-making. One day, after rehearsal, Arturo approached Luigi with a question:

"Luigi, you're a great violinist. You're good enough to be a famous virtuoso in your own right. I'm most grateful that you've always been with me. You've been one of the cornerstones of a fine orchestra. But, Luigi, I'm disturbed to see you make so many terrible grimaces and so many pained expressions. Luigi, are you all right?"

"Look, Maestro, I love you. You are the best and most famous conductor in the world. I'm happy to be with you all these year and do the best I can. I get good pay and live well from my playing. I play the best I can, conscientiously and with zestfulness. But, Maestro, I have a confession to make. I know I'm a good violinist. Yes, my faces reflect a lot of pain. I must tell you honestly, Maestro, my heart is not in it. I hate music!"

---

79. MYSTERY OF THE SILVER DOLLARS

A priest and a nun left a monastery and convent respectively to enter into wedlock. They set up a household in a suburb of their fair city.

The ex-padre worked as an accountant in a bank. The ex-nun spent her time as a housewife.

After a few months the former nun noticed a gallon jar in her husband's closet partially filled with bright silver dollars.

She saw the jar again six months later and noted that it was almost full of bright silver dollars.

That night she asked her husband: "John, I cleaned your closet today. There's a jar of silver dollars there. A few months ago there weren't so many. I didn't know you collected silver dollars. Tell me about it."

"Honey, I have a little confession to make. Those silver dollars represent the savings I'm realizing by being married to you. While a priest, every time I knew a nun, I gave her a silver dollar. Now, every time we make whoopee, I put a silver dollar in the jar."

"What?" burst the nun, "you gave a silver dollar every time you went with a nun? All the fathers ever gave me were special blessings!"

---

80. THE POWER OF DREAMS

Back in early 1945, the three major allied powers, the U.S.A., Great Britain and the U.S.S.R. were decisively winning the war. A conference was scheduled in Yalta, a city on the Black Sea, where the three powers would divide up the conquered countries among themselves.

President Roosevelt, Prime Minister Churchill and the Russian leader, Josef Stalin, met the first evening and celebrated their imminent victory over Germany and Japan.

The next morning at 9:00 A.M., before the formal meeting began, the illustrious leaders held a press conference. President Roosevelt led off the press conference by making this statement to Churchill and Stalin: "Last night I had a most remarkable dream. God made me president of the whole world."

Not to be outdone, Churchill exclaimed: "How coincidental! Last night I had a dream too. God made me prime minister of the universe."

The reporters present clearly recognized these as one-upmanship opening ploys to jockey for a more powerful role in world affairs and especially the new world about to take shape. They turned their attention to Josef Stalin to see how he would upstage his rivals.

Stalin stroked his mustache thoughtfully for a few moments. Then he slowly said to his celebrated guests: "Tut, tut, gentlemen. I don't recall having made such rash promises."

---

81. WAITING IN LINE

In Moscow, Russia, back in the early 1960's, a man got into

a line to buy bread. The bakery was nowhere in sight at the end of the line. The man struck up a conversation and made friends with another man in line.

After two hours in line, the conversation turned to the Russian political and economic situation. As time wore on, the new friends fixed the blame for the scarcity of foods and the other needs of life. They decided that culpability lay with the Russian leader, Kruschev.

A little later one announced to the other: "Hold my place in line. I'm going to get that bastard Kruschev."

An hour later the man returned to claim his place in the bread line. His new friend asked: "Well, did you kill Kruschev?"

"No! That line is longer than this one."

---

82. I DIDN'T WRITE IT!

A teacher was giving her class a test. One of the test questions was: "Who wrote King Lear?"

One test paper was turned in by a student named Johnny. To that question he simply wrote in "I didn't."

When the teacher saw this answer, she sternly asked: "Johnny! I asked you who wrote King Lear. What kind of answer is this?"

"Honest, teacher, I didn't write it," Johnny protested.

Furious, the teacher phoned Johnny's father. "Look, Mr. Janski, I asked your son who wrote King Lear. Do you know what he answered? He said 'I didn't!'"

"Hold on teacher," Mr. Janski countered. "I know Johnny is a little rascal. But he's very honest. If he says he didn't write King Lear, you can take his word for it. He didn't write it!"

---

83. ROBBING PETER TO PAY PAUL

Harry was a little strapped for cash. So he approached a friend, Paul, and asked: Paul, can you loan me $20 for a week?"

"Sure," answered Paul, handing over $20 to Harry.

At the end of the week, Harry was still financially embarrassed. So he approached his friend Peter and asked: "Peter, can you loan me $20 for a week?"

"Sure," answered Peter and gave $20 to Harry. Thus, Paul was repaid.

But again, the following week, Harry was still financially strapped. So he borrowed $20 from Paul again so that he could repay Peter. The following week Harry was still short, so he again borrowed from Peter to repay Paul. This went on for several weeks.

Then Harry hit upon a bright idea. He arranged a meeting of Peter and Paul with himself. Then he said: "Look fellows, I've been getting $20 from each of you and in turn giving it to the other. Why don't you two exchange the $20 between yourselves and leave me out of it?"

---

84. ONE UPMANSHIP

A couple of friends were always topping each other in never ending attempts at one-upmanship.

One day Charles said to Calvin: "Calvin, someday you'll die."

"Yes, someday I must die."

"They'll bury you six feet underground."

"Yes, that's what they do."

"You know, Calvin, grass will grown on your grave."

"Yes, Charlie, that usually happens."

"A cow will probably come along and eat that grass."

"That could very well happen."

"You know, Cal, that grass is going to go through that cow. You know what I'm going to say when that happens?"

"Charlie, I can only guess."

"I'm going to say, 'Calvin, how you have changed!'"

Whereupon Calvin took the stage: "Charlie, someday you gonna die."

"Yes, I must die too."

"And you know, Charlie, they'll probably bury you six feet under."

"Yes, that's the way it is done."

"Charlie, grass will grow out of your grave too."

"Cal, that usually happens."

"And do you know, Charlie, a cow will probably come along and eat that grass."

"Yes, that could happen."

"That grass is going to go through that cow. And do you know what I'm going to say, Charlie, when I see that coming out of the cow?"

"Cal, I haven't the slightest idea what you'll say."

"I'm going to say Charlie, you haven't changed a bit!'"

---

85. CIVIL RIGHTS

During the Negro civil rights movement, many sympathetic Northerners descended upon the South to help the blacks in their quest.

One such team was carrying on a campaign in a Mississippi metropolis. The team, composed of several blacks and several whites, went into a diner to eat. They all sat down at a table together.

When they were settled, instead of a waitress, a big hulk of a man came to the table. "We don't serve niggers here."

"I'm happy to hear that," retorted a white team member. "We don't eat them either."

---

86. PATRONIZING A WHITE BARBER SHOP

A court ruling was announced that accorded blacks access to

white beauty and barber shops.

In Alabama, a young black went the very next day to a white barber shop and ordered a shave. The barber glared at him and began stropping his razor. Then he made a flourish with the razor, and a piece of paper he had tossed into the air suddenly was two pieces floating to the floor.

The barber then lathered his black patron's face and let it soak. Then he proceeded to strop the razor again. He then visually inspected the cutting edge. His black patron was quaking noticeably.

Then the barber approached the barber's chair, holding the razor menacingly in front of the lathered black's throat. Then he said: "Black boy, tell me, what do you think about civil rights?"

His black patron stammered: "I think white folks should have them too."

---

87. SOUTHERN VACATION

A priest went on an extended sabbatical. He went to the sunny warm clime of Southern Alabama and stayed in a country inn. He started the practice of taking long daily walks.

After a few walks, a black youngster began accompanying him. Warm and interesting conversations attended these strolls. The father became fond of the negro boy. They became fast friends.

About a month later, the priest was satisfied he had made a convert. So he broached the matter to the youngster: "Son, you'd be a good Catholic. Why don't you go to church with me this Sunday?"

"No siree, Father! It's bad enough being a nigger down here."

---

88. SOUTHERN VACATION: II

On one of his walks down a country lane, the same priest met a young girl of perhaps ten years. She was leading a monstrous cow. They exchanged greetings.

Sizing up the situation of a small girl leading a huge cow as odd, the priest asked: "My child, where are you taking this animal?"

"This cow is bulling. I'm taking her to the bull to get bred."

"But, my child, couldn't your father do this?"

"Oh, no sir. Only the bull can do that."

---

89. HOW TO GET OUT OF A FALLING AIRPLANE

One Saturday morning, a U.S. Air Force general was reviewing one of his fighter squadrons on the parade grounds. He stepped up to a pilot and asked: "Captain, what would you do if your plane's electrical system failed and it began rapid loss of altitude?"

"Sir, I'd eject."

"How would you eject if the electrical system was out? The canopy would not retract."

"Well sir, I'd eject through the canopy."

"You idiot," said the general, "The impact would kill you instantly."

Turning to the captain's co-pilot he said: "Lieutenant, what would you do?"

"Sir, I'd go through the hole the captain made."

---

90. TWIN BEDS

A married couple had twin beds a few feet apart in the bedroom. On a particular night, the wife departed her bed for a visit to her hubby. On the way over she stubbed her toes on her husband's hobnailed boots and let out a yelp of pain.

Her hubby embraced and soothed her with: "Did my darling hurt her little toesy woesies? Poor little toesy woesies."

In an hour the wife arose to return to her bed. Again, she stubbed her toes on the boots and let out a yelp of pain.

"Why in hell don't you watch where you're going?" admonished her husband.

---

91. THE BIRDS AND THE BEES

Garson came home from a 3-year stint in the U.S. Army, most of it on duty in Vietnam. His father had been in the army too, but, unfortunately, died in an accident ten years before. Thus, when he arrived back home, there was only his mother and 12-year old brother.

His mother took him aside and said: "Garson, you've been away three years. Your little brother has come along. I think it's time he learned about the birds and the bees. Would you do this little duty as he has no father to guide him?"

"Yes, mom, I think I can get this message over to him."

Later, Garson called to his young brother: "Chet, come here. I gotta explain you something."

"Chet, remember when we had girl parties before I left?"

"Yes, Gar."

"Do you remember what we did to them in the garden?"

"Yes, Gar, I remember."

"Well, Chet, mom wants you to know that birds and bees do that too."

---

92. DREAMED YOU WERE MINE

A young man resided in a certain area of Los Angeles. One evening he espied the most beautiful woman he'd ever seen. She was so attractive he followed her until she went into an apartment building.

So betaken was he that on the very next day, he waited outside her building until she put in an appearance. This was a long wait as she did not come out to dusk. He followed the beauty again. She went to a nearby street where, to his dismay, she went with a man who stopped in his car.

The young man sat on a nearby park bench, bemoaning the loss of someone who had struck his heart's fancy. Lo and behold, he was still there over an hour later when the same car pulled up. She departed the car and stood while he gazed upon her beauty. But, alas, a few minutes later, another car stopped and picked her up. This happened a few more times. The moonstruck young man caught on. The lovely girl was a prostitute.

Despite the young man's rude awakening, he continued to observe the stunning beauty for nearly a month. Then one day he announced to the lovely prostitute that he loved her: "Darling, I worship you. Will you marry me? I'll make you very happy."

To which the prostitute replied: "Get lost Buster! I only make love for money. If you want to make love to me, it'll cost you $100.

The young man began approaches almost daily. He was constantly rebuked even though he was warm and complimentary.

After a couple of months of expressing unrequited love, he made an extraordinary admission to the prostitute: "Oh, darling! I dreamed I had the most wonderful time with you last night. I ravished you twice."

"You enjoyed me twice, right Buster?"

"Yes, you seduced me twice. These were the most blissful moments of my life. You really are a great lover. You enjoyed me as much as I enjoyed you. I want to marry you. I'll make you a very happy woman."

"That'll be two hundred bucks, Buster."

"But darling, you made love to me willingly."

"I only make love for money. You fork over $200 Buster or I'll sue you!"

The prostitute became a one-woman collection agency. The young man was equally adamant that she willingly made love.

The prostitute sued. And then came the day in court.

The prostitute recited her case to the judge, seeking court costs and triple damages. Then the young man told the judge that in his dream, the prostitute had made love willingly. In turn, she denied willing love, saying she made love only for money.

The judge rendered his decision: "I'm going to find in behalf of the plaintiff. I'm awarding her damages triple her professional fees. But I make this stipulation: She must dream that she was paid."

93. WHY DO YOU CHASE THAT MAN?

A certain fellow, walking down a street in his city, saw a man sprinting at top speed toward him. He was surprised to see a close friend sprinting in hot pursuit. He was shocked to see the aggressive behavior and terrible mood of his friend. The man being chased passed. He reached out and grabbed his friend.

"Scottie, why do you chase that man?"

"Do you know what that bastard told me to do," his friend gasped? "He told me to kiss his ass!"

"And you ran so hard to do that?"

94. WHAT'S IT LIKE TO BE DRUNK?

A father and his son were in an airport waiting area for a forthcoming flight. While sitting, the son asked his father: "Daddy, what's it like to be drunk?"

"Son, a drunk person loses a sense of balance. His movements are erratic. And his judgement is off. For instance, a drunk often sees double. You see those two men sitting over there. A drunk might see four men."

The lad vigorously patted his father's thighs: "Daddy! Daddy! There's only one man sitting over there."

95. KEEPING LIONS AWAY

A train stopped at a station and took on new passengers. One of the passengers sat down by a man. Only a few moments later, the new passenger began jabbing and poking his finger into the air rather jerkily, but with deliberation. Annoyed, the older passenger asked his seat companion: "My good man, what are you doing?"

"I'm bursting air bubbles," responded the new passenger while continuing to poke his finger spasmodically.

"Why should you burst air bubbles?"

"Oh, that keeps the lions away."

But, my good fellow, there isn't a lion within a hundred miles!"

"Very effective, isn't it?"

96. HOPELESSLY LOST

A salesman was seeking out a back country store located in the wooded hills of Tennessee. There were no street signs, road names or route numbers on the dirt roads he was motoring on. He searched and he searched, but he could not find the general store he was seeking. After miles and miles of back roads, he realized he didn't know where he was or where he was going. By and by he came to a house. A boy was out front leaning on a hoe.

The salesman stopped and asked: "Do you know where Hurd's General Store is?"

"No, mister, I don't," the boy replied.

"Can you tell me where this road leads to?"

"Mister, I don't know."

"You see that road turning off to the left up ahead. Where does it lead to?"

"I see the road, Mister, but I don't know where it goes to."

"How about that road on the right?"

"Mister, I don't know."

"Well, son, where does this road come from?"

"Mister, I don't know."

Exasperated and frustrated, the salesman said: "Son, you don't know very much, do you?"

"I know one thing, Mister. I sure ain't lost."

97. MAKING EXTRA MONEY

A cotton farmer on the high plains of West Texas got a bright idea! In his younger days, geese were used to weed the cotton. The geese thrived on weeds but would not touch the cotton plant because of its contents of a rank toxin called gossypol.

Chemical weeders had taken over from the geese, but the farmer figured the geese were worth it. Herbicide chemicals cost a lot of money. Geese cost little to nothing. They lived off weeds and grains of which he had plenty. But the big bonus: goose down was fetching over $60 per pound.

So the farmer bought a thousand goslings just before spring. But he soon ran into little problems, among which was that of distinguishing between a female goose and a male gander. All goslings looked alike.

He thought his county agent, a college-educated fellow, could guide him. Thus he phoned him: "Clint, this is Jordan. I just bought a thousand goslings. I can't tell a goose from a gander. Can you guide me so I can tell the difference?"

The county agent didn't know either. So he gave some quick off-the-cuff advice: "Jordan, why don't you just put all the goslings on the range and let them figure that out for themselves?"

98. RETIRING AN OLD ROOSTER

A farmer had a huge flock of hens from whence he obtained

food for his table and had eggs, broilers and fryers left over for the market for an extra income.

His rather large flock was serviced by a single rooster who has getting along in years, ten to be exact. One day he reckoned he would replace the rooster with a younger one.

He went to a neighbor who bred a line of purebloods. He picked out a nice rooster ánd paid his neighbor a premium. He brought the rooster home and put it out with the flock.

A rooster doesn't survive to ten years because he is dumb. The old rooster had grown quite wise to the ways of the world and his owner.

When the new rooster showed up on the scene, the old rooster greeted him: "Welcome to my harem, young feller. Make yourself right at home."

So the young rooster squandered his youthful energies visiting as many hens as he could. The old rooster rested up. A few days later the old rooster spotted the farmer on his rocking chair on the porch. He went over to the nigh exhausted young rooster and challenged him: "How about a race, young feller?"

"Beat you anytime old man," crowed the young rooster. So the older but fresh rooster took off toward the house. The young rooster could neither catch nor surpass the elder rooster. The old rooster steered a course around and around the house just ahead of the young rooster. About the third round the farmer became quite aware of the chase.

He watched the old rooster run as if for his life. He watched the young rooster close behind striving mightily. After observing a few more rounds, the farmer arose, snatched the young rooster, took him to a chopping block and axed his head off. "Damned neighbor's still selling me queers," he snorted.

99. WHAT MAKES YOU SO SMART?

An Irishman boarded a train. He took a seat beside a gentleman. Later he realized he was sitting next to a Jewish fellow. A conversation ensued during which the Irishman was struck by the extraordinary intelligence and acumen of his seat mate.

"Why are you Jews so damned smart?""

"We eat schmaltzed herring."

"Schmaltzed herring? Where can I get one?"

"I happen to have a few with me."

"Will you sell me one?"

"Certainly!"

"How much does one cost?"

"A hundred dollars per."

The Irishman forked over a hundred dollar note. The Jewish fellow forked out a herring from a jar. The Irishman immediately began consuming it.

About half way through the fish, the Irishman exploded: "Hey, this fish isn't worth a hundred dollars!"

Responded the Jew: "You see, it already begins to make you smart."

---

100. TRUE PARTNERS

Two Jewish fellows, Nathan and Bernard by name, owned a thriving delicatessen. Bernard worked from 7:00 A.M. to 3:00 P.M. Nathan worked in the deli from 3:00 P.M. to 11:00 P.M.

One afternoon Nathan came to work. After about half an hour he realized he had left some important papers at home which had to be filled out and postmarked that day. Bidding an assistant to take over, Nathan drove home to get the papers.

When Nathan arrived home, he noted his wife's car parked in its usual place. He went to the library and retrieved the crucial paperwork. He didn't see his wife. He looked for her. Nowhere was she evident. Then he went upstairs to their bedroom, thinking she might be taking a nap. Opening the door gently, he saw his wife in bed with his partner, Bernard.

Nathan broke into a fit of laughter exclaiming: ''You Bernie? You? Me, I gotta, but you?''

---
101. HOW TO BUY CARPETING

Three Jewish partners had a thriving rug store on a busy thoroughfare in mid-Manhattan in New York City. They had signs up perpetually that said: ''Going out of business sale,'' and ''last days of sale.''

They sold at very low prices. But their buying techniques justified their ultra-low prices and earned them handsome profits. For instance, one day the three went to downtown Manhattan to a Belgian rug importer who had called them about the arrival of a new shipment of fine Oriental rugs.

The partners descended on the rug showroom and started filling out an order pad. The importer greeted them and thanked them for making such a substantial order, just over a hundred thousand dollars.

Then the unexpected happened. One of the partners made an offer for all the rugs. It was too bad and offer to be accepted: ''I know your wholesale prices add up to over $100,000. Tell you what! You drop the price for the lot to $65,000 and we'll give you cash right up front, right now.''

The importer demurred: ''My cost is greater than that. I could give you $10,000 off for cash on the spot. Otherwise I'm content to wait on payment per regular trade terms.''

''That's no big deal. How about $75,000 for cash right now,'' countered the partner.

''Look, as a final offer, I'll sell the whole lot to you for $87,500 cash.''

His two partners motioned the bargainer into a conference: ''Izzie, why do you offer him cash? You know we don't have that kind of money available. And why should you bust your chops and waste our time trying to beat him down. You know we won't

be paying for the rugs anyway.''
"I don't want that he should lose so much money."

---

102. A QUESTION OF PRICE?

A man walked up to a particularly beautiful young woman and asked her: ''Would you to go bed with me for a million dollars?''

"For a million dollars? Yes, for a whole million I would do your bidding."

"Would you go to bed with me for one dollar?'' asked the man.

"One dollar,'' sputtered the lovely young woman. "Mister, what do you think I am?''

"Lady, we've already established what you are. Now it's only a question of price."

---

103. FREE LOVE

A man seated on a bus by a comely young woman struck up a conversation. By and by he asked. "Do you believe in free love?''

"Absolutely not,'' came the emphatic reply.

"Then, lady, how much do you charge?''

---

104. SELLING BELOW COST

A businessman with a general merchandise store posted this sign: "Selling at cost. Invoices available for inspection."

After a few months at selling at cost, a faithful customer sought out Larry, the owner: "Larry, how can you stay in business by selling at cost?''

"Keep this quiet, friend,'' Larry said, "But I buy below cost."

105. HOW CAN YOU STAY IN BUSINESS?

A furniture store advertised: "Everything sold below cost." Sales boomed so much, the sign did not come down.

After more than a year of heavy selling, a customer asked the store manager: "How can you stay in business if you always sell below cost?"

The manager replied: "We lose money on every sale we make. But we make money on the volume."

106. LET BYGONES BE BYGONES

A Jewish gentleman was walking by a theater where "The Ten Commandments" was showing. A huge black came from the movie house, spotted him, grabbed him and began pummeling him.

"Stop! Stop! Whyfore do you beat me?"

"You damned Jews killed Jesus Christ!"

"But that was 2,000 years ago!"

"I just found out about it."

107. TAILOR MADE

A new tailor opened for business. His first customer was his closest friend who ordered a suit made of the finest wool available. He wanted to launch his friend's business with zing and bolster his confidence. The tailor measured him carefully and then announced he'd have the suit ready in two days.

Two days later his friend returned for the fitting. The first thing that became apparent was one leg being shorter than the other. But the friend did not complain. He bowed one leg to conceal the shortness even though he walked like a cripple. Anything to bolster his friend's self-reliance.

Then he tried on the coat. One side was longer than the other.

The tailor's friend simply leaned over to the opposite side so no one would detect the flaw. Likewise, one sleeve was longer than the other. But the friend overcame this error by holding his arm stretched upward. Yet another flaw manifested. The tailor's friend accommodatingly hunched forward. This flaw was thus not detectable.

All hunched over, bowed, contorted and out of shape, the suit fitted excellently. Further, the fineness of the material gave it a dignified appearance.

Rather than offend the tailor, the friend professed pride and insisted on wearing the suit "to surprise his wife."

As he was about to walk out as a cripple, hunchback and contortionist, two prospective customers admiringly noted the new suit.

One of the prospective customers nudged the other: "Look how well he fitted that poor cripple. Anyone who can make a suit to fit a body like that has got to be good."

108. SMOKING AND LUNG CANCER

When Walt Disney's death was announced on the radio circa 1967, I was in my car in New Jersey going to my place of work in New York City. With me was my nine-year old son, Wendell, who was a great fan of Walt Disney.

When the announcement of death was made, my son became very sad. "Daddy, why did Mr. Disney die?"

"He died of lung cancer."

"Daddy, what causes lung cancer?"

"Cigarette smoking."

My son burst into tears. "Quick, Daddy! Let's go back home. We have to tell mommy to stop smoking."

109. MONEY FOR THE BLIND

A man was walking down Central Park West in New York City. He noticed something very odd. A sign proclaimed: "Help me, I'm Blind." But behind the collection cup was a fellow reading a newspaper.

"How can you say you're blind if you're reading a newspaper," asked the walker.

"Oh, I'm not blind. I am sitting in for my friend."

"Your friend? A blind man should make his own collections. Why isn't your friend here? "

"Didn't you hear? Amadeus is premiering on Broadway. He went to see it."

110. A RABBI TAKES A CONFESSION

A rabbi went to visit a priest in a church near the synagogue. The priest was taking confessions. So the rabbi sat nearby, overhearing the confessions being taken. He was particularly struck by the number who confessed: "Father, I have fornicated."

The father usually responded with: "How many times did you fornicate?" To which the response was on this order: "Father, I have fornicated three times since the last confession."

"May our Father in heaven forgive you. Put $5.00 in the collection plate, please."

The priest received an urgent telephone call. He turned to the rabbi: "Could you sit in for me for awhile?"

"Happy to," responded the rabbi.

The very next confessor said: "Father, I have sinned grievously. I have fornicated."

"How many times did you fornicate, my child?"

"Three times, father."

"We have a special on fornication today! We're charging a

very low price of only $5.00 for three times. Please put it in the collection plate on your way out.''

111. MY FAVORITE SUIT

A man called on his doctor quite frequently with migraine headaches. No matter what the doctor did or prescribed, the headaches continued. After a couple of years the doctor informed him: ''I think I can solve your problem. If we castrate you, it should end your headaches.''

''Doctor, I feel like suicide. Anything is better than death.''

So our sufferer underwent an operation and, behold, he no longer had headaches. A few months later he passed by a clothing store and was elated to find displayed in the window his favorite suit. He went inside and saw a salesman.

When he asked to see his favorite suit, the salesman hesitated: ''Sir, I'd like to sell you that suit. But with your build, the pants would pinch your genookies and cause severe headaches.''

112. A GRACIOUS HOSTESS

A pair of salesmen for an irrigation company on the high plains of West Texas had to oversee setup and initial use of the systems they sold. As most systems were for a square mile or a whole section of land, the sale was usually for around a quarter million dollars.

On one March day they were tied up until after dark supervising the installation of an extensive system. Then they headed back to their home base in Amarillo some sixty miles away over a lot of dirt roads.

On the way back they encountered a rather rare method of irrigation in their area: Mother Nature delivered a deluge followed by a slow, cold rain. Their auto became stuck in the mud. They surveyed their plight and decided the situation was hopeless. They decided to remain in their car for the night, starting the engine as necessary to keep the car interior heated. But.....

When they turned the lights out, they noted a row of lights perhaps a mile down the road. They felt there was a residence there, and perhaps they could fare better there than in the car. So they got out and started slogging through the mud and drizzle toward the lights.

As they approached they saw that the row of lights was the elaborate entrance way to a mansion. They walked under a huge gate and proceeded to the palatial home.

At the door one of the salesmen pushed a handsized button which set off some chimes which played lovely tunes from a bygone era. Soon a charming and lovely lady, perhaps in her early fifties, appeared, noted their wet and muddy condition, and motioned to them to enter a side door.

"You gentlemen have quite obviously had an unfortunate situation with your car. How may I help you?"

"Our car got bogged down in the mud about a mile from here. We didn't relish the prospect of spending the cold night in the car."

"You're most welcome to stay with me. Get stripped and get yourself showered in the bathroom. I'll bring you some dry clothes."

After their shower, a couple of luxurious bath robes were handed to them through the door. "These belonged to my late husband. Please use them. I'll prepare dinner for you. I have two guest rooms ready for you. And I'll clean your clothing and shoes so they'll be ready for you in the morning.

The salesmen were impressed and touched. The warm and thoughtful hospitality overwhelmed them. Their instant hostess was good-looking and most accommodating.

They enjoyed a five-course dinner that could more properly be described as a feast. Then the hostess showed them to their rooms where she provided each with pajamas and a cheerful good night.

One of the salesmen was heartened by such warmth, attention

and generosity. He betook himself to thank their hostess and offer his assistance with their dirty and wet clothing. The hostess was in the laundry room. He offered his help only to be politely refused. A conversation ensued and kisses and embraces followed. Then the salesman spent an hour with the hostess in her bedroom.

At the end of his visit, the hostess asked for his name and address. Taken aback by the request and not wanting to risk his wife finding out about his tryst, he gave her the name and address of his partner who was single.

A few months later, his single partner greeted him happily and said: "Wolfie, do you remember that widow who took us in when we were bogged down?"

"Yes, Bill, I remember her well. Has she contacted you?"

"No, but something very strange has happened. I'll never understand it. She died the other day and left her entire estate to me."

113. A SEXY PARTNER

A businessman to his catankerous partner: "Joe, you're very sexy today!"

"How do you figure that?"

"You're acting like a prick."

114. HOW TO BE MASTER IN YOUR HOUSE

Fred and his wife of 50 years held their golden wedding anniversary. At the celebration a friend since childhood asked: "Fred, you've never had any backtalk from Cora! How did you manage to wear the pants in your house?"

"I reckon it's like this," Fred responded to his buddy and several bystanders. "When Cora and I went on our honeymoon, I had a new horse and buggy. We took off and hadn't gone even a mile when that horse went down. I got out and jerked that horse up by the bridle, shook my finger at it and shouted: 'That's once!'

"We had gone only a little way farther when that horse fell again. I jerked that horse up again. I shook my finger and shouted: 'That's twice.'

"This time the horse made it more than a mile down the road and went down again. I got out, shook my finger at him and shouted: 'That's three times!' I took out my pistol and shot that horse dead.

"Cora started ranting and screaming at me. She was even going to call off the marriage and go home. This went on for maybe five minutes. When she stopped, I said 'Have you had your say?' and she said 'yes.' I shook my finger at Cora and shouted, "That's once!' I haven't heard a peep out of Cora since."

115. ON BECOMING A FATHER

A couple of partners had a thriving fur business. Among their employees was a lovely bookkeeper. Relations between her and both partners developed. A few months later Norma told both partners she was pregnant and didn't know which of them was the father.

When she started becoming heavy with child, the partners got together and sent her to Florida rather than suffer embarrassment with their friends and wives. They set her up in a house under comfortable circumstances.

When she called and said birth was imminent, one of the partners flew down to be with her.

When the partner returned, he was dressed in black. His curious partner inquired: "How's Norma? How's the baby? And why are you dressed in mourning?"

"Norma's fine. She had twins. Mine died."

116. THE BIG FISH STORY

A Boston fish cannery had a certain lot of canned sardines on hand. In fact, they were around so long that the owner one day said to an account executive: "There's a thousand cases of sardines we've had on hand for more than a year. Move them!"

The account executive got on the phone to a New York distributor: "I got a real buy for you, a thousand cases of sardines for $4.25 a case."

"You're not kidding me, are you?"

"No, it's on the up and up."

"Ship them right on down."

Immediately the New York distributor got on the phone with a Philadelphia distributor: "I have a thousand cases of sardines for you. I can let you have them for only $5.25 a case."

"Ship them right away."

The Philadelphia distributor got on the phone with a Pittsburgh distributor. I've got a good buy for you, a thousand cases of sardines for just $6.50 a case."

"I'll take them."

The Pittsburgh distributor got on the phone with an Ohio grocery chain: "Look, I've got a thousand cases of sardines I don't need. If you can use them, I'll make you a special price of $7.50 a case."

"As a matter of fact we're in the market for sardines. We can use them immediately."

About a week later a call reached the account executive of the Boston fish cannery whose label was on the cans: "This lot of sardines is rotten."

Came the retort: "You moron! Those sardines aren't for eating. They're for selling."

---
117. YOU MUST SELL LOTS OF SALT!

A retailer went to a salt distributor: "I need a hundred bags of salt. Can you handle it? "

"Can I handle it? Look at those bags. All are salt."

"Gee, you stock lots of salt."

"You've seen nothing yet. Come to the basement." There the salt distributor showed thousands of bags stacked from floor to ceiling on both sides. Then he took his customer to the second and third floors which were stocked similarly.

"Gosh, you must sell a lot of salt," the customer remarked.

"What, me sell a lot of salt? I don't sell much salt. If you want to meet someone who sells lots of salt, you should meet that salesman who calls on me."

---
118. WHY DIDN'T YOU AND ETHEL HAVE ANY CHILDREN?

At his fiftieth wedding anniversary, the host was asked: "Raymond, you and Ethel never had any children. Why not?"

"I courted Ethel for six years before we were married. The evening before the wedding, we were together. I felt so horny I asked her to go to bed with me then and there. She really blew up. She gave me so much backtalk and made me feel so miserable, I haven't asked her since."

---
119. A TOUR WITH ST. PETER

A group of new arrivals were being taken on a tour of heaven by St. Peter. He highlighted points of interest.

"Over here, we have the Baptists. Over there are the Episcopalians," he said.

After walking further he said: "Over there are the Presbyterians and over there are the Methodists."

After a while he shushed the group. He kept them quiet for a long time as they walked. "O.K., we can talk again."

"St. Peter, why did we have to be so quiet back there?"

"Oh, those are the Catholics. They don't believe anyone else is up here."

---

120. WHY DON'T YOU TAKE YOUR MEDICINE?

A woman took her twelve-year-old son to the family doctor because of a severe cold. The lad was so stuffed, he could hardly breathe. The doctor duly examined the youngster, but one thing was rather obvious to both mother and son. The doctor suffered a severe cold too. He blew his nose often. He used a hanky to wipe away a constant drip. His nose was red raw. He spoke hoarsely with a nasal twang. And he was breathing through his mouth like his client. Yet, the physician wrote up a prescription and advised: "Keep him home for six to eight days. Give him his medicine every four hours. Keep him resting in bed or on a sofa as much as possible. Make sure he eats well. He should be cured and in school within ten days."

The prescription was filled. Mother attempted to administer her son's first dosage. She was met with refusal and resistance.

"Why aren't you taking your medicine? The doctor ordered it special for you."

"Mom, I'm not going to take that stuff. If it's so good, why does the doctor have a cold?"

---

121. IT'S AN HONOR TO DIE FOR YOUR COUNTRY!

A British captain whose company was about to go to the front lines made a speech to his troops to bolster their morale: "It's an honor to die for your country," he said as he wound up his pep talk.

A hand went up from the ranks. "Yes, soldier?" acknowledged the captain.

"Sir, wouldn't it be a bigger honor to make the enemy die for his country?"

---

122. COMMANDING A COMPANY

During the First World War, a Jewish merchant was conscripted into the Russian Army. Because of his education he was given the rank of captain. After 30 days of intensive training, he was sent to the front in charge of a company of soldiers.

Arriving at the front, his company encountered withering fire from unseen Germans. At least a dozen died and many more were wounded while getting to cover. Then artillery started dropping explosive shells. Several more men were killed.

"Retreat," came the order from Captain Feinstein. And his company ran to the rear in view of other companies and their commanders.

Soon other officers took charge of the retreating men and directed them back to the front. They took Captain Feinstein in hand.

"Captain Feinstein, you're a disgrace to the Russian Army. You are a coward. You ran from the enemy. There's only one way to redeem yourself and restore an officer's honor. You must take your life."

With this admonishment the officer gave Captain Feinstein his pistol and departed the room with some fellow officers.

The officers were discussing the captain's situation. One said: "Izzie has been in the army only 31 days. What does he know about our code of honor. Let's quietly forget this."

The other officers nodded assent. But just as the officer was about to go into the room, a shot rang out.

All the officers rushed in. There stood the captain, pistol in hand but grinning: "Sorry gentlemen, but I missed."

123. WHY DID WE EAT THE FROGS?

A couple of boys were walking across a field. A toad frog hopped away from their path.

"Jamie, I bet you $10 you haven't got what it takes to eat that frog, guts, bone, skin and all?"

"I'm no piker," said Jamie who then caught the frog and, with difficulty and distastefulness, ate the frog. His walking mate gave him $10.

They walked on and spotted another toad frog. Jamie said: "Bobby, I bet you $10 you haven't got nerve enough to eat that frog."

"I'm no piker either," said Bobby. He caught and consumed the frog. Jamie returned the $10 to him.

About half an hour later, both boys started vomiting and felt terribly sick. Said one to the other: "Tell me, why did we eat the frogs?"

124. TERRIBLE TRUCK DRIVER

A trailer truck driver pulled up to a diner and went in to have a meal. He was served at a table and had finished his meal. While he was drinking coffee and having dessert, four burly black-jacketed motorcyclists with fancy helmets sat themselves down at an adjacent table.

Matters immediately took a sadistic turn. A motorcyclist came to his table, picked up the cup of coffee and poured it over his head. Another joined in and pushed the truck driver's head into his dish of ice cream. The truck driver didn't resist or voice a single word of objection. Yet another motorcyclist turned the truck driver's chair over, sprawling the truck driver onto the floor. The fourth motorcyclist kicked him while he was down. Still, the truck driver did not respond.

The truck driver got up, quietly paid his bill and left.

"That guy sure ain't no fighter," one of the cyclists blurted aloud.

"He ain't a good driver either," a nearby waiter chimed in. "He just ran his huge tractor/trailer over four motorcycles."

125. BRAIN POWER

One student roommate to another: "Scotty, I just discovered an easy way to have more brainpower. This package formula contains lecithin, choline, zinc, RNA and DNA which I got from the health food store down the street."

Scotty: "Now you're getting smart. They sold me the same supplements over six months ago and I've been on them ever since."

Buddy: "You have, eh? Well, that shoots down that big discovery."

126. HAVE A CIGARETTE?

Smoker to new acquaintance: "Have a cigarette?"

New acquaintance: "No thank you, cancer isn't my thing."

127. SHE'S GOT ONE

Gift shop patron to sales girl: "Perhaps you can help me select a gift for my wife?"

Sales girl: "Happy to help you. How about this cute little figurine?"

Patron: "She's already got one."

Sales girl: "How about this necklace?"

Patron: "She's already got one."

Sales girl: "Here's a new perfume from Paris."

Patron: "She has perfume too."

Sales girl: "How about this music box?"
Patron: "She already has one."
Sales girl: "I know just the thing. This book just came out."
Patron: "A book? No, she's already got one of those too."

---

128. NO CHRISTMAS GIFT

Friend: "I've gotta get my wife a Christmas present. Have you any ideas?"
2nd Friend: "Sorry, pal, but I have no ideas."
1st Friend: "Well, what are you getting your wife this Christmas?"
2nd Friend: "Nothing at all."
1st Friend: "Well, why not?"
2nd Friend: "I gave her a chess set last Christmas. She hasn't used it yet. Until she does, why should I get her another gift?"

---

129. WHAT IS YOUR OPINION ON SEX?

Poll taker: "Sir, what is your attitude on sex?"
Interviewee: "I want you to know I'm very strongly in favor of it."

---

130. SNEAKING OUT THE BACK DOOR

President Reagan and Nancy slipped the secret service guards, took their limousine and went for a drive in the Maryland countryside. They drove for an hour and had a flat tire. President Reagan is a self-sufficient man. So he went to the trunk of the car, took out the jack, jacked up the car, took a tire tool, removed the hub cap, and took the lugs off the right rear wheel which had the flat.

As President Reagan took off each lug, he carefully placed it in the hub cap. When he removed the spare tire he dropped it to the ground. It bounced a couple times, hitting the hub cap on the third bounce. The tire capsized the hub cap, spilling the lugs which rolled into the sewer through the grating.

Ron surveyed his situation and decided he needed road service and more lugs. Directly across the street was a state asylum for mentally affected people. He proceeded to it with the idea of calling for road service.

As President Reagan neared the place, he was aware of an inmate in the window near the main door. He was surprised to hear the inmate's voice calling to him: "Mr. President, I suppose you want to use the phone to call road service?"

"Yes," Ron responded. "How would you know?"

Inmate: "I've been watching you since you stopped. May I suggest that instead of calling road service, you remove a lug from each of the three remaining wheels and mount the spare with them."

Reagan: "That's a bright idea! Tell me, why should a bright fellow like you be here?"

Inmate: "I'm here for being crazy, not stupid."

131. WHERE'S JOE?

Hey, where's Joe?

He just went to the psychiatrist.

Psychiatrist? That's dumb. Anybody who'd go to a psychiatrist should have his head examined.

132. A GOOD CONVERSATIONALIST

A good conversationalist is someone who'll patiently listen to everything you have to say.

133. LET'S OPERATE!

Surgeon to assistant: "Quick, let's operate before the patient gets well."

134. I'M GOING TO SHOOT YOU, YOU AND YOU!

A private in the U.S. Army was given 15 years in the stockade for brutally assaulting his commanding officer.

After five years in the stockade, he was eligible for parole. He went before three officers of the stockade which comprised the parole board.

"If we parole you, what are you going to do?"

"I'm going to get me an inner tube, make me a bean flip and shoot you, you, and you!"

"Parole denied. See you in a year."

A year later the same inmate came before the same board.

"If we grant you parole, what are your plans?"

"I'm going to buy a car."

"What are you planning to do with this car?"

"I'm going to take off a tire, remove the inner tube, make a bean flip and shoot you, you and you!"

"Parole is denied. You're eligible again in another year."

A year later the same board convened for the same inmate to consider his parole application.

"If we grant you parole, what will you be doing?"

"I'm going to buy a car."

"What are you going to do with a car?"

"I'm going to carry my girlfriend in it."

"Where are you going to take your girlfriend?"

"To a nice grassy picnic area in a park."

One of the officers nudged the questioner and whispered: "I don't think we should embarrass him with intimate questions."

2nd Officer: "Please bear with my line of questioning."

"What are you going to do when you get your girl to a grassy area in the park?"

"We're going to have a picnic dinner."

"And then what did you plan to do?"

"I'm going to lay her on the grass."

"Yes, and what are you going to do while she's laying on the grass?"

"I'm going to take off her panty."

1st Officer: "I think you've gone far enough. He's got the right idea. Let's grant him parole."

2nd Officer: "Please, just another question or two."

"What are going to do after you've removed her panty?"

"I'm going to take the elastic from her panty, make a bean flip and I'm going to shoot you, you and you!"

---

135. A COMMUNICATIONS GAP

In Brooklyn there lived a fierce Mafia chieftain. He headed a gambling and betting syndicate which took in millions of dollars daily.

He was notorious for killing his bookkeepers who seemed to have a predilection for sticking their hand into the till. He was thus always getting new bookkeepers. So it was no surprise that, one day, he heard about a perfectly honest bookkeeper. But there was a catch. He was deaf and dumb and could be communicated with only by sign language. So the chieftain made a generous offer to the deaf and dumb bookkeeper, one he couldn't refuse. Then he hired someone who could communicate both by voice and with hands and fingers just to interpret for him.

He gave the bookkeeper mountains of cash each day to count and prepare for distribution to his henchmen and investment portfolio. But, at first, he counted the money himself before passing it on to the bookkeeper. Everything came out very exact and precise. This went on for a couple of months. Then the chieftain only did a precount once in a while. Then the precounts dropped off to once or twice a year. Despite the millions of dollars in cash handled each day, everything came out right to the last penny.

After twelve years, the chieftain counted a certain day's receipts as $17 million plus. But, heresy of heresies, the bookkeeper accounted for exactly $3 million short. So Mafia chief got the interpreter.

"Go get the bookkeeper," he said in a rage. The interpreter duly summoned the bookkeeper.

"Tell him his accounting is three million dollars short. Tell him I want that three million and I want it right now!"

The interpreter made a series of gesticulations and signs. The bookkeeper made a long series in return.

"Boss," the interpreter said, "he says he is a very honest man. He wouldn't take your money. He knows how harshly you deal with dishonesty and he likes his job."

"Tell the bookkeeper he took the $3 million and he'd better come up with it right away or I'll kill him."

Again there was an exchange of gesticulations and finger signs.

"Boss, he still says he's an honest man. He wouldn't take your money. You pay him well, far beyond his needs, and he likes working for you. Please reassure him of your trust."

"Tell him he took $3 million. I know he did it. Either he comes up with three million right away or I'm going to blast his brains out," the hot tempered chieftain blurted out, pulling his pistol from his shoulder holster.

The bookkeeper quaked. When the chieftain's message was delivered he gesticulated and said in sign language: "Boss, I'm very sorry I was tempted. I took the $3 million, put it in a box and stashed it among several other boxes in the basement. Please forgive me."

"Boss, the bookkeeper insists that he is honest, that he

wouldn't take your money, that he is happy working for you, and that, after all these years of honest service, you don't have guts enough to blow his brains out.''

136. WHAT'S THE MOST IMPORTANT PART OF A BICYCLE?

Professor to students: "What's the most important part of a bicycle?"

"The front wheel," replied a student. "You can even ride that one wheel as in a unicycle."

"The handlebars. Without them you couldn't guide the bike," submitted another.

"The brakes! Without brakes you'd crash and hurt yourself."

And the answers went on and on, each student naming a different part.

The professor then supplied his own answer: "The most important part of any bicycle is always the part that's missing."

137. PLEASE KEEP THE LITTLE BOY QUIET

A New York City businessman was scheduled to be a keynote speaker at a trade conference in Chicago. His practice was to write the speech, then develop an outline, and work from the outline. His speech became fixed in his mind in this way.

By the time he had to depart for Chicago, he still had not written or outlined his speech. "I'll do it on the plane," he kept assuring himself with each successive deferment.

When he got on the plane to Chicago, he immediately took his writing materials to compose the speech. But a disturbing complication arose simultaneously. A little boy began noisily romping in the isle.

"Will you be quiet if I give you a dollar?"

"Yes sir!"

The dollar was given, but the little fellow continued playing boisterously as before. The businessman simply could not compose himself, much less a speech under the circumstances. So he appealed to the hostess.

"Do you think you can get this lad to be quiet?"

"I'll try sir."

Quiet ensued, and the businessman devoted the rest of his trip to writing and outlining a speech of which he was proud.

At the end of the trip the businessman called the hostess, pressed a $5 bill into her hand and said: "I thank you for keeping the little fellow quiet. But tell me, how did you do it?"

"Oh, I just told him to play outside."

138. INFIDELITY

An Air Force officer was stationed in England, leaving his wife and two children in the States. He had not been there many months when the wife received positive evidence that he was going out with an English girl.

The wife fired off a letter to her hubby telling him in no uncertain terms how she felt about marital infidelity. As a P.S. she wrote: "What's she got that I haven't got?"

Came hubby's letter: "Honey, she doesn't have a thing you haven't got. But she's got it here."

139. 105-YEAR-OLD TAKES AN ANNUAL PHYSICAL

A 105-year-old woman went to a physician for an annual physical.

"You're in great shape," pronounced the physician. "I hope to see you next year."

"Doctor, I hope to see you next year! Statistics don't show any 105-year-olds dying, but they sure show lots of 52-year-olds dying."

140. 96-YEAR OLD VISITS DOCTOR

For the first time in his life a 96-year old man went to a physician, complaining of excruciating pains in the abdomen. Upon being greeted by the physician the 96-year old said apologetically: "Doctor, if I had known I was going to live so long, I would have taken better care of myself."

141. ATHEIST SWEARS ON BIBLE

An atheist received a construction contractor in his home to estimate the cost of adding a new bedroom to accommodate a child now on the way. The contractor gave him a quote: "This additional bedroom will cost you $22,500. But it must be cash as the work is performed. I work for 20% less than other contractors, but I can do it only by getting my money as I go. Do you swear I'll be paid?"

"I swear on this bible you'll be paid as you require it," the atheist responded.

When the contractor departed, his wife reproached him: "How can you conscientiously swear on my bible you're going to pay him when you're an atheist?"

"Honey, the Bible is the safest place I know to hide things," her husband said as he opened the Bible displaying $100 bills secreted in its pages here and there. "I've got 250 of these C notes hidden in your Bible."

142. FUNNY MONEY

An actor came to a certain city with his troupe. He had a penchant for beating plush hotels out of room charges. He did it on this order: He would deposit with the hotel manager for "safekeeping" $10,000 in amazingly real-looking $100 bills which he also used as play money. At the end of the engagement, he would skip out, leaving the bills in the hotel safe.

On this particular occasion, the nicest hotel was selected for their stay. Upon arrival, the actor insisted on dealing directly with the owner only. He asked the owner to deposit $10,000 in his safe for him. The owner readily assented, and one hundred bills of $100 denomination were passed to him bearing a real bank wrapper showing the contents to be $10,000. He ordered his staff to give the actor and his troupe real VIP treatment.

But the hotel owner was in deep financial troubles. A contractor was threatening to put a lien on his hotel for $10,000 if he didn't come up with the cash that day for work performed several months before. The hotel owner couldn't raise the money, so he decided "to borrow" the actor's deposit from his safe.

The hotelman took the $10,000 in real-looking play money and gave it to the contractor. The contractor had problems of his own. He took the $10,000 straight to a building supply company to pay against his accumulated bills. The building supply owner was planning a lavish shindig for the many contractors who patronized him and others whom he hoped would patronize him.

The building supply owner called the owner of the fanciest hotel in town and arranged a super duper affair.

"How much of a binder would you like to have?" the building supply owner asked the hotel owner.

"$10,000 will do," the owner said.

So that selfsame pack of phony $100 bills was soon back in the hotel owner's hands where he, in great relief, deposited it back into his safe for safekeeping.

---

143. ONLY ONE LESSON NEEDED

A wealthy lady went to a pet shop. She communicated to the owner: "I want a smart dog. I want one so smart that if I give him a lesson or routine just once, he will follow it."

"I have just the dog for you, a lovable dog already trained to do a lot of tricks. He'll do anything if shown only once.''

A sale was made. The lady took her very cute little dog home to her second floor condominium. She hadn't been home for more than 30 minutes with her ingratiating pet when it went to her expensive bearskin rug and pooped on it.

Furious that her new dog did this to her, she wanted to give it an immediate lesson. She gathered up the cute little fellow and, saying "bad dog, bad dog," threw it from the second floor window. She was satisfied the dog would behave after such harsh punishment.

The next day at about the same day the new pet went to the lovely bearskin rug and pooped again. Again the owner was furious. But her dog had, indeed, learned the lesson. It ran and jumped out the window on its own.

144. POLACK GETS SICK

A Polish gentleman worked at a factory where he was appreciated for his good manners and hard work.

One day the worker became sick. His foreman sent him to the company nurse. The nurse, not being able to resolve the problem, referred him to the company physician in a nearby office.

Early that afternoon the Polish worker arrived home two hours early. The first thing his wife witnessed him doing was tossing an obviously expensive package into the waste basket.

"Darling, why are you home so early? And why should you throw that package away?"

"Look, my love, it's like this. Today at work I got sick. The foreman, he sent me to the nurse. The nurse, she sent me to the doctor. The doctor, he got to make a living, so he make me a prescription. The drug-store man has to live too. So I get the prescription filled. Me, I want to live too, so I throw away the prescription."

145. NO TROUBLE ON THIS HILL

A trucker came down a long grade in descending a Vermont mountain. He had the brakes on so much they were smoking from the friction and heat. Seeing a turnout about halfway down the mountain, he pulled in. There was a service station there, so he decided to refuel the truck.

The service station was attended by an elderly lady Vermonter who insisted on pumping the truck full of diesel all by herself. To make conversation, he asked the lady: ''Does anyone ever have trouble on this hill?''

''No, mister, I been here over 30 years and I never saw anyone have trouble on this hill. But hundreds have had terrible troubles when they reached the bottom.''

146. COMPLAINT ABOUT MONEY

The wife made a request to her hubby for additional money with which to feed themselves for the week.

Hubby: ''What are you doing with all the money I give you for food? Seems to me like you could feed an army on the money you get.''

Wife: ''Honey, did you ever calculate the cost of getting yourself up to 240 pounds?''

147. THE EARTH IS ROUND

Hamar: ''Mose, I just found dat de earth is round.''

Mose: ''Everybody knows de earth is flat and rests on a turtle's back.''

Hamar: ''Aha! And what do de turtle rest on?''

Mose: ''Come on now, let's not meddle in dat turtle's business.''

148. MAKING AN IMPRESSION

A young swashbuckling executive was given a big promotion. With the new job came a new office. When he occupied the office, not all the necessary equipment was working or installed. Though it didn't work, his new phone was an awesomely marvelous electronic complex with great capability.

As he was admiring his new phone's features, a beautiful young woman in work attire knocked and entered his office. Trying to make an impression upon the lovely young woman about his important station, he held the phone in a speaking position and was loudly laying out a plan, obviously to the company president.

Deigning to take notice of the young woman who stood before him, he said: "Hold on a moment, sir. I have a caller," as he held his hand over the speaker.

"And what may I do for you, Miss," he said to his lovely visitor?

"Sir, I'm with telephone installation service. I've come to put in your phone lines."

149. THIS IS WHAT I GET PAID FOR

An inmate of a state institution for the mentally disturbed was given the job of mopping up water in a basement by the superintendent. He went to the basement and was mopping away. After a few hours, an institutional supervisor happened by.

"George, what you mopping for? Can't you see that it does no good as long as the faucet is on?"

"Boss sent me down here to mop 'er up, not to turn off any faucet."

150. ARE THE GREATEST JOYS FREE?

"Josh, you're tipsy. And you're still drinking. You know the greatest joys in life are free."

"What do you mean the greatest joys in life are free? You think they give this stuff away?"

151. THE ONE THAT GOT AWAY?

A poor Catholic needed food for his family table. He knew the fish were running. So he went fishing at a nearby lake.

He fished and fished. No matter what bait he used, he got not a bite. Getting desperate to catch fish for the family table, he said a prayer to God: "God, give me a huge fish. If you do, I'll put $10 in the collection plate next Sunday."

Soon the fisherman had a huge strike, one so strong it almost pulled him into the lake. He began wrestling with the pole and pulling mightily on the line. Then he whispered: "God, perhaps you'd be happy if I put just $1 in the collection plate on Sunday?"

Suddenly, the fish broke off the line. The fellow then wailed: "God, couldn't you take a little joke?"

152. I KNOW HOW TO HAVE A BABY

Seven-year-old Alene to six-year-old Susie: "Susie, I know how to have a baby."

Susie: "That's nothing! I already know how not to have a baby!"

153. BRIDE OF CHRIST

I was lecturing before about 30 Carmelite sisters in a convent on the subject of health. I was deep into diseases, their causes, and natural, remedial steps that would overcome them.

An older nun, obviously a Mother Superior, asked me: "How do I get over this arthritis?"

"I suggest, as a starter, that you fast for 21 days, taking only water as needed, and give your body the opportunity to autolyze the deposits of offending calcium salts."

"What? Starve myself for 21 days?"

The audience went into a titter with my answer: "You call yourself a bride of Christ, who fasted 40 days, and you can't do without food for half that long?"

154. WHAT WOULD YOU BUY WITH FIVE DOLLARS?

Uncle Otho came to visit his nephews and nieces. It was the occasion of Robbie's fifth birthday. All were ensconced around a TV set and hardly even acknowledged his presence. All but one, that is, little Robbie. He left the TV set, sensing the possibility of another gift.

"Hi Uncle Otho," he said in greeting him.

After some conversation, it turned in this direction: "Robbie, what would you do with $5 if you received it as a gift?"

Being fresh off TV fare which he observed for six to eight hours daily, at least a fourth of which was advertising, Robbie answered: "I'd buy lots of Tampax."

"Tampax?" exclaimed the uncle. "Why would you buy Tampax? What would you do with it?"

"I'm not sure how it works. But it comes with directions. If I use Tampax according to directions, I can go dancing, swimming, skating, horseback riding and do lots of other things."

155. PHALLIC WORSHIP

A young art collector bought some African, carved-wood art objects. Among them was an oversized carving of a penis. He elected to display this on his living room mantle.

One day while visiting the museum, he met a lovely young woman who was similarly disposed to objects of art. He invited her to his home to view his private collection, an invitation that she accepted.

After viewing some of the art together, the young man received a telephone call. He asked his guest to continue her viewing while he answered the phone. He was on the phone for quite some time. By and by she came to the unusual carving on the mantle.

When the host finished his phone conversation, he rejoined the lovely art lover. She asked: ''What do you call that wood carving on the mantle?''

''Oh, that's a phallus.''

''That may be a phallus or whatever you call it, but I'd hate to tell you what it looks like to me.''

156. PIGEON RACES AIRPLANE

There was the time when we depended solely on propeller airplanes for air transport between cities. In New York City a pigeon lover was quite proud of his carrier pigeons. He could dispatch them to other cities with great reliability.

He was telling a friend about their speed and reliability in such a boastful way that it ended in a bet. ''My pigeons fly at 80 miles per hour. I can still get messages from here to Washington, D.C. faster than air express.''

''I'll bet you a C-note your pigeon can't beat me to Washington!''

''You just lost a hundred! You'll take an hour to get to the airport from here. You'll spend at least half an hour getting set and boarding the plane. With flying time of one hour for the 240 miles, at least ten minutes spent in taking off and about ten minutes in landing and getting into the airport as well as another hour getting to the rendezvous point, you'll need nearly four hours. My pigeon can fly from here to the rendezvous point in three hours.''

Despite this, the bet was on. The pigeon was released, and the friend took off in a taxi for the airport.

Who do you think won the race?

The friend won handily. The pigeon walked.

157. WHY DO I GAIN WEIGHT, Case I

As a health mentor to Harvey and Marilyn Diamond, I am mentioned many times in their book, FIT FOR LIFE. Because of this and my own publications, thousands call me seeking guidance in health matters. Some are downright funny.

For instance, a lady called me and told me how disappointed she was with the diet. Her friends were losing weight and she was still gaining.

I questioned her carefully as to what she ate. She ate raw vegetables and fruits, none of them cooked. All fruits and vegetables were low calorie or negative calorie. Negative calorie foods, almost all vegetables, require more energy for their digestion than is derived from them.

Exercise? She walked a few miles every week and danced once or twice weekly.

I figured she just had to be losing weight!

I questioned her further.

''You're positive you eat nothing besides fruits and veggies?''

''I eat my fruits and veggies faithfully, after every meal.''

158. WHY CAN'T I LOSE WEIGHT, Case II

I received a call from a distressed lady who, having read Fit For Life at the behest of a friend who lost lots of weight, began the program herself. She could not lose weight. Instead, she gained over 12 pounds during the two months she was on the Fit For Life program.

So I questioned her carefully. Fresh raw fruits and veggies? Yes! No conventional foods? Absolutely not! Avocados? Sometimes. Nuts and seeds? Not at all. Exercise? Yes, at least four times a week to a Jane Fonda video, plus more walking.

I was mystified.

"Mrs. Adams," I stated, "if this is all you're eating, and you're exercising, you must lose weight. There's no way you could be gaining."

"Sir, that's all I'm eating, and I am exercising. I've gained 12 pounds in the last two months."

"That's impossible, I assured her. You'd be the first person ever to gain weight. Are you on medications?

"No."

A flash of inspiration: "What do you use for salad dressing?" Mayonnaise."

How much?"

I get my mayonnaise from a health food store and I finish a quart jar about every three days."

159. I PRACTICE FOOD COMBINING

Fit For Life implores us to combine our foods, if more than one is eaten, so as to be compatible in digestive chemistry. This is taught in the celebrated course I created in the nutritional, behavioral and health sciences which the Diamonds completed.

When I'm lecturing I go into details about what combines with what and the principles that apply.

At one lecture during questions posed by the audience, a listener assured the audience: "I certainly practice food combining, and I don't understand splitting hairs about it. I combine just about everything I can get my hands on."

160. DADDY, COME QUICK!

When my daughter, Cynthia Ann, was one year old, my wife and I got her a pet dog. We called the dog Snoopy for he was forever exploring things.

About two years later, on a nice restful Sunday, my daughter excitedly awakened me from a sleep on the sofa: "Daddy, come quick! Snoopy has his wee wee stuck to another dog."

161. MAKING A SKILLED DIAGNOSIS

A suffering man made a call upon a physician. The physician observed and then asked the client details about the symptoms. He did this several times as he ostensibly had other business, but actually consulted diagnoses guidelines in reference books.

Befuddled, the physician asked the client: "You ever had this before?"

"Yes, a few years ago."

"Well, you got it again."

162. HAPPINESS

As a landlady told a friend:

"There was a knock at my door. A handsome young fellow whom I took as a student at the college stood at the door. He came in. He didn't say a word. He caressed me. He kissed me. Then he made me happy. He rested a few minutes. Then he made me happy again. Then he left without saying a word. I still don't know what he wanted."

163. FOOT REFLEXOLOGY

A young man met a lovely young lady with whom he made a dinner date. After dinner the couple went to a concert. Then the young man was permitted "to drive her to the door."

But, at the door, he offered her a foot massage which he had already determined she liked very much. She accepted and he thus gained entrance to her apartment. Within an hour they were both amorous.

Afterwards the young woman asked him: "Why did you offer to massage my feet when all you really wanted was to make love?"

"I always start at the bottom and work my way up."

---

164. MANICURING AWAY LONESOMENESS

A macho salesman went to a barber shop for a shave before calling on a major business client.

While he was being shaved, a ravishing young beauty approached him: "Sir, would you like a manicure?" Having had no intention of getting a manicure, he could not refuse the lovely manicurist.

As the manicure got underway he began to converse. She responded. Soon he said: "I'd really like to know you better. Can we make a dinner date for this evening?"

"No, I'm married."

"Why don't you call your husband and tell him you're going to spend the evening with a girl friend?"

"Tell him yourself. He's shaving you."

---

165. THE PURPOSE OF DEEP BREATHING

I was an exhibitor at a health fair in San Francisco. There were hundreds of exhibitors. As I had two assistants, I took a tour of the many exhibits.

At one exhibit, four exhibition spaces were taken by a single exhibitor, an Indian Yogi who sat atop some pillows, smiling and bowing at every passerby. I acknowledged him with a return bow and smile that caused him to laugh. I could not help but notice his huge paunch, really an extraordinary example of a prolapsed belly.

As I paused I was accosted by an American attendant. He handed me some brochures about the fellowship and invited me to learn more about it in an ashram in the city. Then he plied me with different practices of the fellowship. One of these practices was deep breathing. He noted my large chest and said: "You're a shallow breather. In deep breathing you make excursions with your belly, not your chest. "Look," he bid me as he drew a few breaths. His abdomen expanded considerably with each inhalation. There was no chest rise or fall.

"Aha," I exclaimed. "I see the benefits of deep breathing. Your guru must do a lot of it. That would account for his huge belly."

---

166. MY HUSBAND HAS ALZHEIMERS

"My husband has Alzheimer's disease," asserted a lady to her visiting neighbor.

"What is Alzheimer's disease?"

"That's where you forget almost everything."

"Your husband forgets? Just this morning he remembered to bring me some tomatoes from your garden. He remembered my name. And he remembered to tell me I looked as beautiful as ever."

"That's just the point. He keeps forgetting who he's married to."

---

167. DIRECTIONS TO A HOUSEWARMING

Joseph Silverstein, who had been born in the Bronx and lived there for 42 years, had a new house built on Long Island. After two weeks of living in the new home, he went back to the Bronx to visit friends and to make an invitation to attend his housewarming party.

To one friend, Jerry Golden by name, he made an invitation. Jerry asked: "I accept, but how do I get to your house, Joe? I have no car."

"You get a Long Island Railroad train. Get off at the Hempstead station. Take a bus to East Meadow. Get off at the Elm Street stop. Go three blocks up Elm Street and turn right onto Beeline Drive. Just walk two blocks to 714. Then you take your elbow and ring my doorbell."

"I understand your instructions, Joe, but what's this bit with ringing your doorbell with my elbow?"

"Jerry, don't tell me you're coming empty-handed."

168. PREEMIES

The first-born to the modern American couple is likely to be a preemie. The first born-usually comes five to seven months after marriage.

169. SHOULDN'T WE GET MARRIED?

A young couple had lived together for six years. One day the lovely young companion asked her lover: "Honey, isn't it about time we got married?"

"What? And spoil a beautiful relationship?"

170. THE LAW IS THE LAW

If a man observes a woman dressing or nude through a window, he is arrested as a peeping tom.

Should a woman see a man dressing or nude through his window, he is arrested for exhibitionism or indecent exposure.

171. THE FIRST COMMANDMENT

A chairman of the board who was also the chief executive officer at a certain manufacturing firm ran the company with an iron hand. The board of directors was merely a rubber stamp to his decisions.

A vacancy developed on the board. A really bright young go-getter with a good track record with the company and already functioning at the executive level was nominated by the board. But, at the election, the elderly chairman campaigned so hard against the dynamic young leader that the nomination was withdrawn.

One of the newer directors said to another board member: "Why did the chairman object so vehemently to this promising comer? He is already capable of becoming our chief executive officer."

"The chairman believes very strongly in the first commandment. You know, 'Thou shalt have no other gods before me.'"

172. AROMA THERAPY

When a certain couple were married, the wife undertook to live the life style of her husband, which was strictly fruits, nuts, seeds and vegetables with little or no cooked food. However, when she and her husband visited food shops and super markets, she hankered after the old foods, namely donuts, bread, pastries, hamburgers, french fries and other forbidden fare.

As the wife had vowed not to consume junk foods, she did not insist on purchase or eating of the forbidden fare. But she did get her husband to agree to what she called "aroma therapy." She would smell the no-no foods for a minute or two and walk away saying: "Aroma therapy has done the trick for me."

This practice went on for over a year. One day the wife was particularly desirous of sexual union. When her husband arrived home, tired, dreary and rather energyless that day, she smothered him with kisses, began fondling him and made her demand when he was totally stripped of his smelly work clothes. He demurred, saying he was too tired and out of sorts. When she made a rather insistent new approach he responded.

"Here," he said, handing her his discarded briefs, "have a little aroma therapy. That should do the trick."

173. TWO KINDS OF COWS

When my son, Wendell, was six, we took a tour of a nearby dairy from which our milk was delivered.

He asked the owner, who was showing us around, what kind of cow was black and white. "That's a Holstein." Then he wanted to know what kind of cow was light tan. "That's a Jersey."

Later Wendell told the owner: "There's 23 Holsteins and 36 Jerseys."

"That's right," the owner confirmed.

When we got home he was excitedly telling his mother about the place our milk came from, the electric milkers, the calves, the neck yokes, and other features.

"Wendell," I asked, "tell mommy the two kinds of cows the farmer has."

Came the knowing reply: "He has mommy cows and daddy cows."

174. SMART BOY

My son, Martin, was an extraordinarily bright child. At three he could articulate sentences and formulate questions perfectly and logically.

On a visit to my printer, Martin took a tour of the plant, courtesy of the owner, as I proofread copy in the typesetting department.

When I had finished, the owner commented as to Martin's keen perception and understanding. "How old is Martin?"

"Three," I replied.

"Only three? He speaks as well as a five- or six-year old."

"Yes," I said, "and he can already add figures in the billions in his head."

"This I gotta' see. I never heard of a three-year old adding figures in the billions in his head.

"Martin," I commanded, "Tell Mr. Anderson how much are three billion and two billion."

"Five billion."

---

175. SIGN LANGUAGE

There are lots of signs in men's toilets. Below are some that I recall.

"Aim well. Janitor can't swim."

"We aim to keep this place clean. Your aim will help."

"A man's ambition is mighty small, who'd write his name on a toilet wall."

Sign on a swimming pool: "I won't swim in your toilet if you won't tinkle in my swimming pool."

---

176. HONEST BOY

A boy, standing on a diving board, pulled down his bathing suit and emitted a stream of urine which made quite an trajectory before landing in the swimming pool below.

The lifeguard yelled: "I'm going to have you arrested for urinating in the pool."

The boy yelled back: "Arrest me? What about those in the pool? At least I'm honest."

177. NOT A COMPETITOR

Next to the giant Chase Manhattan Bank headquarters in downtown New York, there was a hot dog vendor. He had a thriving business.

An old friend who frequently bought his hot dogs rushed up and demanded: "Angelo, loan me $10 until tomorrow."

"I sure would like to do that, paison, but I have a little agreement with the bank. They agreed not to sell hot dogs and I agreed not to make loans."

178. AIN'T GONNA' DIE!

A beginning golfer's ball landed atop an ant hill. He took a swing at the ball and missed, killing perhaps a thousand ants.

He took another swing and missed. He swung again and again, killing thousands upon thousands of ants. The golf ball still remained atop the ant hill and only two ants survived. Said one to the other: "If we want to survive, I think we better get on the ball."

179. A PENGUIN STORY

A refrigerator truck had 50 penguins to deliver from a ship to the Bronx zoo on a sweltering July day.

In upper Manhattan the truck conked out including the refrigeration system. The truck owner, also his own mechanic, began trying to diagnose and repair the truck. After an hour of sweating he became desperate on behalf of his precious cargo.

A man who was watching asked if he needed help. "Do I need help? I have to get these penguins to the zoo in a hurry. I can't abandon my truck in the street. I'll pay you well to take them to the zoo for me. Will you do it?"

"What's involved?"

"Just carry this penguin and the rest will follow. Here's $200 for expenses and compensation."

"O.K., I'm on my way," he said as he picked up the designated penguin. The good samaritan left with all the penguins following him faithfully. The truck driver began anew to fix his truck.

After about four hours the truck driver got his truck running again. He was going to the zoo to see if the delivery of the penguins had gone well.

But, as he was starting to go, the man who was to take the penguins came back, holding one and the rest following.

"You were to take these penguins to the zoo," admonished the truck driver. " Didn't you make it? "

"Yes, we made it. These penguins had a great day at the zoo. I had so much fun with them I'm not going to take a dime. Here's the $120 I had left after the subway fares, zoo entrance fees and four boxes of fish."

180. THE AMISH DELIVER

In the Amish country of Pennsylvania, an Amish farmer had a son who got married. The son and his wife stayed with him "until a good farm could be had."

A few months later, an adjacent conventional farm was up for auction to the highest bidder. The Amish farmer knew the farm well. With its closeness, this was just the farm for his son. He decided to bid for it.

On the day of the auction, he and his wife attended the auction. The bidding started at $25,000 but quickly mounted. The Amish farmer topped every bid submitted. When the Amish farmer nodded assent to a bid of $44,000, there were no further bids. He was declared the buyer.

"Brother Schneiderhan, how did you intend to pay for this farm?"

"With cash! Wife, go home and get the bucket."

A short time later the wife returned with a sealed bucket. The farmer opened it and the auctioneer counted it.

"Brother, there's only $40,000 in this bucket."

"Wife! You brought the wrong bucket."

181. HAND WARMER

On a very cold day, a farmer had to do repair work on his truck in the open air. Within 30 minutes his hands were so cold they would no longer function. He came inside where his wife was-- in bed.

"Darling, could you warm my hands between your legs?"

"Of course, honey," the wife responded, placing his icy cold hands and fingers between her legs. They were speedily warmed.

A little later he came back with icy cold ears. She cupped them with her hands. A little later yet he came in with a nose in danger of frostbite. She warmed hubby's nose with her bosom. Then he came back and complained of icy cold cheeks. She assented but said: "Honey, isn't it about time we warmed your hands again?"

182. HONEY, WHAT IF I DIED?

A wife asked her husband: "Honey, what if I died? Would you marry again?"

"Let's be straightforward and frank about this. I probably would, just as you probably would if I died."

"Honey, should you remarry, would you give your new wife my furs?"

"I most likely would."

"Would you give her my diamonds?"

"Yes. That wouldn't make any difference to you if you were gone."

"Would you give her my golf clubs?"

"No! She can't use left-handed clubs."

---

183. SPRAYING FOR FLIES

A housewife was spraying her kitchen for flies. She opened her mouth to yawn, and a fly flew in. She turned the sprayer around and doused the fly inside her mouth with spray. She became so sick, she called an ambulance and was taken to the hospital.

At the hospital she received visiting neighbors. One asked: "Viola, what illness caused you to be here?"

"Helen, a fly flew into my mouth. He darned near killed me."

---

184. HALLOWEEN TAKE

On Halloween dozens of youngsters dressed in rather frightening costumes knocked on my door for trick or treat. I always treated with fancy candies bought for the occasion. Then I became health-oriented and felt the children deserved something better than candy. I bought a case of the finest and largest Washington red delicious apples I could get at the wholesale market. They were known as the Wenatchees.

As the evening came on also came the inevitable ringing on my doorbell. Most received the apples into their bags and went on their way. But one youngster, even before I had the door closed, said aloud: "An apple. Yuk!" Then he threw the apple on the ground.

The next morning I went outside to see at least a dozen of those giant red beauties thrown on the lawn, walkway and roadway.

---

185. WHAT KIND IS THIS ONE?

My wife and I took our daughter, Cynthia, to the Bronx Zoo. She was just four. And she was very curious about every animal.

She asked at each stop: "Daddy, what kind is this one?"
On a trek between cages we encountered a Chinese family
with their child of approximately her age. Came the question:
"Daddy, what kind is this one?"

---

186. MY DUMBEST MISTAKE

Husband: Make my dinner. I'm tired of waiting.
Wife: Make it yourself. I'm leaving. Marrying you was the
dumbest mistake I ever made.
Husband: Come on, now. Make my dinner. Don't make me the
victim of your dumbest mistake.

---

187. PARENTAGE

In a certain community a young man dated a lovely girl. He
brought her home to visit his parents.
"Mama, meet Rachel. Papa, this is Rachel. We're planning to
be married."
The father asked: "Rachel, are you the daughter of Ellen who
is married to Joseph?'
"Yes, I am."
Later, the father pulled the son aside: "Son, I hate to tell you
this, but you can't marry Rachel. She is your half-sister."
That ended that relationship. But soon, another lovely beauty,
Helene, was introduced to the parents.
The father asked: "Is your mother Sarah who is married to
Harry Wellman? "
"Yes sir, Sarah is my mother and Harry is my father."
Later, the father pulled his son aside again: "I regret to tell you
this again, my son. But you should go no further with Helene.
She, too, is your half-sister."
Disappointed and exasperated, the son went to his mother:
"Mama, I brought two wonderful girls here as my prospective

brides. In each case Papa told me they were my half-sisters. What am I to do?''

''Don't pay any attention to your Papa, my son. He doesn't know it, but he's really not your father.''

---

188. YOU BE NICE TO ME!

There was a knock at a certain householder's door. Upon opening the door, a large man confronted him in a gruff, demanding, hostile and threatening voice:

''You're Danny Smith. I'm Skullcracker Jones. I'm here for Lemmon's Department Store. You owe us $856.00. You haven't paid us anything in five months. I'm here to collect it all. If you don't pay up now, you'll regret it. Go get our money so I can be on my way.''

''Look, Mr. Jones! Once a month I put all my bills in a hat. I pick out some and pay them. Either you be nice to me or I won't even put your bill in the hat.''

---

189. WHY IS A DOG SO FAST?

My 7-year-old son, Velton, and I were running up a very steep hill. His dog came running past us on the way up.

''Velton, how can a dog run up a hill so much faster than we can?''

''The dog has four-wheel drive'' was my son's response.

---

190. BLIND DATE

On a certain campus in Oklahoma, it was a common practice of male students to call the girls' dorm and propose a date to whichever coed answered the phone.

On one occasion this transpired: A male student called the

dorm, and a sweet young voice answered. She readily accepted his proposal for a date.

"My buddy wants a date too. We can make it a foursome. Can you bring someone with you?" asked the young man.

"Just a moment. I'll ask my room mate," was the response. She went to her room and asked: "Ellen, would you like to go on a date with me?"

"No," came the curt answer.

"Why not?"

"Don't you know I'm a virgin?"

"Since when?"

"For two months already."

191. LEG EXPERTISE

In preparation for a test, a college student spent most of the prior night studying the intricacies of zoology, particularly ornithology.

When entering the classroom the following day, he found ten stuffed birds on stands, all having sacks over them except for the legs.

The professor told the students that the test would consist of identifying the ten birds, their species, genus and habitat from examining the legs.

To the student all the bird legs looked alike. He studied them carefully. He thought about it. He became disgusted, then angry. He stalked up to the professor's desk and protested: "What a stupid test! How can anybody tell the difference between those birds when all have legs that look alike?" Then he turned to walk out of the class.

"Young man," interrupted the shocked professor, "what's your name?"

The enraged student pulled up his pants to the knees saying: "Go ahead. You see my legs. You tell me."

---
192. NO JEWS FOR SURE

During the second world war, a proper Southern lady's daughter turned 18. She desired to give her a memorable coming-out party. There were about forty young women who were friends with her daughter, but, alas, not even a half dozen eligible young men.

Our would-be hostess, Mrs. Warren, got a bright idea. She called an army base about 60 miles away and requested to talk to the captain of the best company of men. She was duly put through to a company commander. ''Captain, I need 35 nice young men for my daughter's coming-out party.''

''That's O.K. with me ma'am,'' the captain replied. ''I'm going to turn you over to the sergeant, and he'll arrange details with you.''

So a young man came on the line and took her name and address along details about her guest requirements and directions to her home. When all was in order, she said to the sergeant: '', please don't send any Jews.''

The evening of the coming-out party, over 40 young ladies eagerly awaited the arrival of a busload of nice young men. By and by, the brakes of a bus were heard. In a few moments there were knocks on the huge plantation doors.

The hostess opened the doors, and in trooped a negro sergeant and 35 strapping negro soldiers. ''Bring on the broads. We hear there's some belly-rubbing to be done here tonight.''

''Sergeant, there must be some mistake,'' protested the hostess.

''I don't think so, Mrs. Warren. Sergeant Goldstein is not known to make mistakes.''

---
193. SLOW!

A gentleman drove to a neighbor's house in his car to pickup a couple who were going to a party with him and his wife. Upon arrival the following conversation took place:

"Floyd, I'm here to pick up you and Ginny for the party while my wife get's ready at home."

"You should have brought Delia with you. My wife is so slow, she's late for everything. I daresay she'll be late for her own funeral."

"That's nothing compared to Delia! She's so slow, she probably won't make it to her funeral at all."

---

194. SEX ON MARS

Two Russian cosmonauts were launched on a trip to Mars. One of the cosmonauts was a lovely Russian lady, Ivana by name. The athletic and handsome young cosmonaut was named Igor.

After a few days they landed on Mars. To their surprise there was life there, including people very much like those on Earth except they were considerably larger, perhaps an average of seven feet in height for men.

They were greeted and shown the sights on Mars. They liked all that they were shown and treated to, especially the trinkets they could take back.

The cosmonauts were back at their capsule together and brought up the subject of sex. Let's see what they're like sexually. Both agreed to explore.

Ivana took a liking for a statuesque Martian and seduced him. But a problem developed. His was no larger than one of her fingers. She communicated this to him. He pulled on his left ear and it immediately elongated to perhaps a foot. She then communicated that it was too thin. The Martian pulled on his right ear and it thickened to perhaps three inches.

Back at the capsule she met Igor and said: "I've just had one of the most wonderful experiences of my life. How did your affair go?"

"It was one of the worst experiences of my life," retorted Igor. "She was as beautiful as a princess. I've never seen a lovelier woman in all my life. But when we came together, all she did was pull my ears."

---
195. GOING TO A DOCTOR

A friend persuaded a lady to try a new doctor. "He's such a wonderful doctor. You'll love him. He has such a wonderful bedside manner. You should make an appointment right away."

So an appointment was made with the doctor.

In due course the appointment came about. She was ushered into the doctor's office where she discussed her problem.

"Get undressed and lie down on the bed," commanded the doctor.

"Doctor, you're highly recommended, but please, not so fast. We hardly know each other."

---
196. THE PIG'S REVENGE

On one of my trips to Korea, my host and I flew with an interpreter to an island south of the mainland. The south of this island is semitropical and is a great resort.

We stayed at a resort hotel in which my host had an interest. A lovely English-speaking Korean lady was one of the partners and managed the hotel. She was Catholic and had an Anglican name of Alice. She was hostess to a military conference which was in progress. Generals and high ranking officers were meeting with top academic military strategists.

On Sunday afternoon the climax of the conference was a barbecue that served a wealth of foods including two pigs which were turned on a spit over coals. Each had an apple in its mouth. As a fruitarian/vegetarian this was gruesome to me.

My host and interpreter joined in the repast. My plate boasted tropical fruits; pineapple, papaya and persimmons being heavy among them.

My interpreter urged me to fill my plate with pork, telling me how delicious it was. Instead of condemning pork eating I told her that I was a fruit/vegetable eater and that, if I ate pork, I would probably get sick to my stomach, vomit it up or get a diarrhea, get a fever and be incapacitated for a day. I told her that, if I ate the pig you might call the results "pig's revenge."

The next morning we wanted to depart but could not give our goodbyes to our hostess. By and by we found that she was ill and in her room. We knocked on her door and an attendant admitted us. She was still abed. She had a fever and a diarrhea. She described these symptoms in English. And she felt too weak to be up and around for which she apologized.

While we were in her room, a local doctor came. He took her vital signs and, in Korean, asked her some questions. My interpreter, in a knowing manner, pronounced her problem as "Alice has pig's revenge."

INDEX TO JOKES

Through Key Words In The Title And/Or Joke

Title of Joke	Joke Number